# Great Western ⟨⟩ Holiday Lines

## in

# Devon

## and

# West Somerset

**Alan Bennett**

Published by
**Runpast Publishing**
10 Kingscote Grove  Cheltenham GL51 6JX

To my wife Josephine

© Alan Bennett
Runpast Publishing
June 1993

ISBN 1 870754 25 5

Printed by
The Amadeus Press Ltd
Huddersfield, West Yorkshire

Road and rail images of the fifties! This could almost be a late pre-war scene, both forms of transport here being heavily laden as they run along the waterside between Cockwood and Starcross. 'Hall', No. 4909, *Blakesley Hall*, is seen here heading a returning Swindon Works holiday train. A classic period-piece, dated 13 July 1957, resonant of the style and character of that vanished, beguiling era.

P. Gray

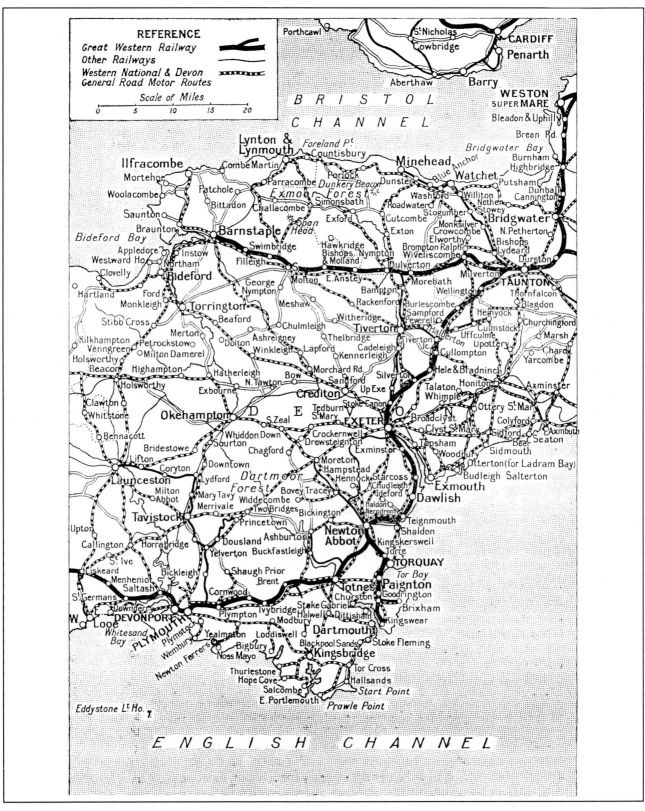

*Front cover:* 'Castle' No. 5059 leaving Goodrington Sands Halt with combined Kingswear portions of *The Royal Duchy* and the Liverpool/Manchester train on 19 June 1961. Although it is 6.40pm there are still quite a few people on the beach and look at those carriage sidings!!

*P. Gray*

*Back cover:* Steam in the nineties! Continuing the GWR tradition, 4500 Class 2-6-2T No. 4561 – an old friend in the West Country – leaves Minehead for Bishop's Lydeard on Easter Saturday 14 April 1993. The station retains much of its former identity thanks to the West Somerset Railway Company, and North Hill, as a backdrop recalls GWR poster work of long ago.

*Author*

# Introduction

The Great Western Railway claimed a decisive double distinction in the years separating our two World Wars. Building on earlier developments, the Company created powerful, evocative imagery for the West Country which was to play a major role in shaping the region's subsequent character and identity. The GWR had quality material to work on, no-one could dispute that, but the inspired creative energy of the Company's publicity department met all requirements and expectations.

This achievement was more than imagery, no matter how creative; it was backed by substantial progress in hard engineering terms, making the 'Holiday Line' a reality at all levels. Given the vital 'marriage' of image and substance, the West Country was set a distinctive identity, which, for better or worse, has had a profound influence upon its social, economic and cultural life. There can be no doubt that the GWR took every opportunity to identify itself with the region, becoming, in effect, a definitive part of that community. Nowhere was this more so than in South Devon, where the identity was total.

Much of the engineering achievement of the twenties and thirties has now, sadly, diminished and one has to look to history, to re-create, for ourselves, the priorities and accomplishments of the past. There are plenty of reminders in the railway landscape between Taunton and the River Tamar to indicate something of the scope and scale of former times, but the atmosphere, character, spirit, call it what you will, of those years can only be appreciated now in words and pictures. Its vital energy has gone, in line with the much reduced role of the railway in the overall life of the community.

This book is by way of a celebration of that vanished era, one of confidence and purposeful expansion,

reflected in intensive timetabling and new works and by continuity on the more leisurely branch services, resonant of another, older England. Goodrington Sands, Clearbrook Halt, Gara Bridge, or that evocative double act, Ingra Tor and King Tor Halts, for example, embodied the GWR no less than prestigious Plymouth, Taunton or Newton Abbot.

Goodrington is, fortunately, still with us, with the bonus of steam trains on the Paignton and Dartmouth Railway. Go there, today, with or without the steam train at the platform, and sample the place. Does the spirit of the GWR linger there, or is it largely sentimentality for long ago; for sunshine, sand and sea? Was it that the GWR image-makers worked too well, or is it images that make the deepest impressions long after fact falls away? Again, could it be that 'Glorious Devon' and 'Smiling Somerset' have since become veritable 'lands of lost content', the GWR's most enduring legacy to the West Country outbidding the technical and commercial achievement? Commercial gain was the obvious driving force behind all Great Western innovation and others now benefit from those earlier initiatives, but what was the most decisive influence of the railway: was it commercial or cultural, was it both, or can they even be separated?

To whatever extent one pursues this theme, if, indeed, at all, it cannot be denied that the Great Western was at centre stage; a decisive influence. This is the essential focus of the book – the Great Western's involvement in creating and actively promoting the holiday industry of Devon and West Somerset.

Alan Bennett
April 1993

# Contents

# Acknowledgements

There are many people to be thanked here.

Firstly, Stephen Mourton for the opportunity to publish the work, and the following, for their excellent photographic contributions: Terry Knight of the Cornish Studies Library, Redruth; Peter Gray; R. C. Riley; Peter Treloar; Michael Mensing; Roger Venning; Pursey Short and Tony Fairclough. Thanks also to the National Railway Museum, York; West Country Libraries, Exeter and Plymouth; the Penzance Library and Courtwood

Film Service, Penzance. I must also thank Margaret Barron for typing the manuscript and, of course, my wife Josephine, for encouraging and helping me throughout the project.

My sincere apologies in the event of my missing any further fitting acknowledgements; I am most grateful for all the interest and effort shown towards this project by everyone involved in it.

'King' No. 6019, *King Henry V* brings the 'down' *Cornish Riviera Express* past Laira locomotive depot, climbing to Mutley Tunnel and North Road on 4 April 1957. Laira was opened in 1906, and was enlarged in 1931. Its allocation included numbers of all main line locomotives – Kings, Castles, Counties, Halls, Granges and Manors for its long distance workings. *R. C. Riley*

The Watchers on the Wall! A fifties family watches the 12.25 a.m. Manchester-Plymouth on a fine summer's day, 14 July 1959. 'Castle' No. 5005 *Manorbier Castle* takes its train along the final section of the sea-wall to Teignmouth. *R. C. Riley*

# Chapter One
# Origins and Development

Whit weekend, 1846, saw the opening of the first stage of the South Devon Railway from Exeter to Teignmouth. *The Exeter Flying Post* celebrated the event in appropriate manner, reflecting much of the character, optimism and boundless energy of that great Railway Age. Progress and change were paramount.

Things have been effected and works done, that within the life of man would savour of romance and such have been the monster trains that have, as it were, flown from hence to Teignmouth and returned from thence to this city . . . Saturday, about noon, was fixed on for the first passenger train . . . and amidst cheering the train started, consisting of nine carriages and having power of two fire engines – the Exe and the Teign, it swept past the west and south faces of the City and suburbs with a velocity that set at nought that of the arrow. Alphington, Exminster, Kenton, Powderham, Starcross and Dawlish sent forth their population to greet the numerous persons in the carriages as the train passed, accomplishing the journey in 43 minutes. On Sundays trains were completely filled and the influx of persons each way was immense. All, however, was surpassed on Monday. It was Whit-Monday – a holiday according to ancient custom – At the station at Exeter, from the hour of seven in the morning it was a most animating scene. The numbers continually increasing in order to take the trip down; indeed, such was the amount that twenty-one carriages were needed to contain them, and it is computed that upwards of 1,500 persons were sent down by the morning train, while about an equal number came up. Language would fail adequately to describe the scene – Yesterday (Tuesday) there were again immense numbers in each direction, the weather continues delightful and "a trip to Teignmouth" is the all-engrossing theme.

Pursuing the theme of 'a trip to Teignmouth', the *Plymouth Devonport and Stonehouse Herald* drew attention to the tourist potential.

There can be no doubt that this salubrious and beautifully situated watering place will greatly benefit by railway communication . . . There are several very excellent inns and a number of lodging houses where every accommodation is afforded the visitor.

Teignmouth had already created an image of a fashionable and select watering place, well before the arrival of the railway, to the extent that sections of the town might well have questioned the 'benefits' promised by the railway. The town had a population of 4,688 in 1831, comparing very favourably with that of Torquay at 4,786, but the railway brought rapid and radical change in the style and pace of life for South Devon as indicated in population figures for the mid-century. Teignmouth grew to 5,149 by 1851, but Torquay in the meantime, had climbed to a figure of 13,767; Dawlish had 3,546 inhabitants whilst Paignton in 1851, recorded a mere 2,746; the twentieth century was Paignton's particular era.

Tourist traffic was no special priority for the early railway interests in Devon. The main line, developed separately by the Bristol and Exeter and the South Devon companies, meeting at Exeter, linked Plymouth in the west with London, Bristol and the Midlands, these works being completed in 1849. Trade and commerce were set to flourish despite the Exeter Canal Company and elements of the local corporation putting up determined opposition to the South Devon's line. There were great hopes for Plymouth as an international trading port and Packet Station, yet whilst the railway was so vital to the prospects of the region, South Devon company policy had been such as to present more than a few definite 'hostages to fortune.'

Decision making in the early stages of the railway in South Devon had a decisive influence on the progress, character and, indeed, limits of all later developments. For this reason it is important to consider the early years and to recognise their significance, not least for tourist traffic.

The Bristol and Exeter Company's circumstances were very different from those of the South Devon Railway, as things eventually emerged. For the former, construction was relatively straight-forward. Their double-track, broad gauge route through a largely level landscape with long, straight sections, presented no great engineering challenge other than a number of cuttings, thence bridging and embanking on the Somerset flatlands, that is, until the climb through the Blackdown Hills on the Somerset-Devon border. Thereafter, the line followed a leisurely descent through the Culm Valley to Exeter.

The South Devon, however, although at first planning double track over its 52³/₄ miles had much harder country to contend with. It had also been "selected with the design of accommodating the largest amount of population in the district." As Company Engineer, Brunel favoured a coastal route to Newton Abbot, thereafter, skirting Dartmoor on an inland alignment via Totnes, Ivybridge and Plympton. He abandoned an earlier idea to avoid Newton Abbot by taking his coastal route across the Teign to the Torquay area and then westward over the Dart and through the South Hams. Having then upset the Admiralty by putting his line along the shore at Dawlish and Teignmouth, thereby exposing it to possible enemy attack, from the sea, or so it was thought, Brunel took on nature and the power of the sea itself. He built a line, immemorable to the traveller by train and part of Devon's emergent seaside mythology, but liable to frequent damage and dislocation in winter-time. The South Devon, again, with Brunel's advice, also adopted the atmospheric system, rejecting conventional steam traction.

Brunel championed the atmospheric system believing it to offer considerable advantages, not only of speed, but smooth riding, the absence of "coke dust and sulphureous smell" from locomotives, and the recourse to heavier gradients. A number of pumping houses along the route provided the power, creating the vacuum in the 15 inch pipes set between the rails thereby drawing the trains along by the atmospheric power. Eight

'Glorious Devon!' – Peter Gray's inspired composition of the branch line railway in the Devon landscape. Fields and farms, villages, woodland, river and railway all contributed to a quintessential rural England. The Kingsbridge branch was a particular delight and the subject of much praise in the pages of GWR publicity works. Here, a 4500 Class 2-6-2T No. 4561 works a late afternoon train to Brent and the main line on 8 June, 1961. Diptford church, or, rather, its spire, can be seen on the skyline, above the trees.          *P. Gray*

Heavy work on the way to Ilfracombe. The 1 in 40 gradient for more than half the gruelling six-mile climb from Braunton to Mortehoe in North Devon saw much evidence of assistance in the form of bankers as seen here in the summer of 1963. 4300 Class 2-6-0 No. 6346 is helped by Ivatt 2-6-2T, No. 41298, with the five coaches of a Wolverhampton-Ilfracombe on 27 July 1963. An unassisted Class 4300 was limited to 190 tons between Braunton, Mortehoe and Ilfracombe; a Southern Class N was allowed 180 tons.          *P. Gray*

# SOUTH DEVON RAILWAY

THE RAILWAY will be OPEN between EXETER and TEIGNMOUTH, for the Conveyance of Passengers and Parcels, on and after SATURDAY, the 30th of MAY Instant.

The First DOWN TRAIN will leave Exeter on Saturday, the 30 h' May, at 12 30 P.M., and the First UP TRAIN will leave Teignmouth at 1 15 P.M.

After Saturday, the 30th May, the following Trains will run daily, viz. :—

## ON WEEK DAYS.

| UP TRAINS. | | | DOWN TRAINS. | | |
|---|---|---|---|---|---|
| Leaving Teignmouth at 7.10. a.m. | arriving at Exeter at | 7.55 a.m. | Leaving Exeter at 8.10. a.m., | arriving at Teignmouth at | 8.55 a.m. |
| 9.10. a.m. | .... .... | 9.55 a.m. | 12.10 p.m., | .... .... | 12.55 p.m. |
| 11.10. a.m. | .... .... | 11.55 a.m. | 2 20. p.m., | .... .... | 3. 5 p m. |
| 1.15. p.m. | .... .... | 2. 0 p.m. | 3 25. p.m., | .... .... | 4.10 p m. |
| 4.25. p.m. | .... .... | 5.10 p.m. | 5.40. p.m., | .... .... | 6.25 p.m. |
| 6.45. p.m. | .... .... | 7.30 p.m. | 7.40. p.m., | .... .... | 8.25 p.m. |
| 8.45. p.m. | .... .... | 9.30 p.m. | 10.10. p.m., | .... .... | 10.55 p.m. |

## SUNDAY TRAINS.

| UP TRAINS. | | | DOWN TRAINS. | | |
|---|---|---|---|---|---|
| Leaving Teignmouth at 7.15. a.m., | arriving at Exeter at | 8. 0. a.m. | Leave Exeter at 8.20. a.m., | arriving at Teignmouth at | 9.15. a.m. |
| 9.30. a.m. | .... .... | 10.18. a.m. | 5.40. p m , | .... .... | 6 25. p.m. |
| 8.30. p.m., | ... .... | 9.25. p.m. | 10. 5. p.m., | .... .... | 10.50. p.m. |

FARES—From Exeter to Teignmouth—First Class, 2s. 6d. ; Second Class, 2s. ; Third Class, 1s. 2d.

By Order of the Directors,

Exeter, 18th May, 1846.

W. CARR, Secy.

\*\* NOTE.—Horses, Carriages, and Dogs, will be conveyed by Railway, and also Fish ; but, for the present, no other description of Goods.

---

### SOUTH DEVON RAILWAY TIME TABLE.
*Corrected to Feb. 1*

#### UP TRAINS.

| | ON WEEK DAYS. | | | | | | ON SUNDAYS | | |
|---|---|---|---|---|---|---|---|---|---|
| FROM | 1,2,3 | Exp. | 1, 2. | 1, 2. | 1, 2. | 1, 2. | 1,2,3. | 1, 2. | 1, 2. p. m. |
| | a.m. | a. m. | a. m. | p. m. | p. m. | p. m. | a. m. | a.m. | p. m. |
| Plymouth .... | 6 50 | 10 20 | 12 0 | .. | 4 50 | 6 25 | 6 50 | 12 0 | 5 25 | 6 25 |
| Plympton .... | 7 2 | .. | 12 15 | .. | 5 2 | 6 41 | 7 2 | 12 13 | 5 41 | 6 41 |
| Ivybridge .... | 7 26 | .. | 12 35 | .. | 5 25 | 7 3 | 7 26 | 12 35 | 6 1 | 7 3 |
| Kingsbridge R | 7 34 | 10 51 | 12 45 | .. | 5 34 | 7 10 | 7 34 | 12 45 | 6 9 | 7 10 |
| Brent ...... | 7 41 | .. | .. | .. | 5 41 | .. | 7 41 | — | 6 15 | .. |
| Totnes ...... | 7 58 | 11 10 | 1 6 | .. | 6 0 | 7 30 | 7 58 | 1 6 | 6 30 | 7 36 |
| Newton ...... | 8 25 | 11 35 | 1 33 | .. | 6 25 | 7 53 | 8 25 | 1 33 | 7 0 | 7 53 |
| Torquay ...... | 8 45 | 12 5 | .. | .. | .. | .. | 8 45 | .. | 7 20 | .. |
| Teignmouth .. | 8 47 | 11 57 | 1 37 | 4 47 | 6 45 | 8 7 | 8 47 | 1 47 | 7 17 | 8 7 |
| Dawlish...... | 8 57 | 12 7 | 1 57 | 4 57 | 6 55 | 8 17 | 8 57 | 1 57 | 7 27 | 8 17 |
| Starcross .... | 9 7 | 12 17 | 2 7 | 5 7 | 7 5 | 8 27 | 9 7 | 2 7 | 7 37 | 8 27 |
| St Thomas (Ex) | 9 22 | .. | 2 22 | 5 22 | 7 22 | 8 42 | 9 22 | 2 22 | 7 52 | 8 42 |
| Exeter ...... | 9 30 | 12 35 | 2 30 | 5 30 | 7 30 | 8 50 | 9 30 | 2 30 | 8 0 | 8 50 |
| Taunton...... | 10 53 | 1 27 | 3 48 | 6 53 | .. | 10 5 | .. | 3 48 | .. | 10 5 |
| Bridgewater .. | 11 15 | 1 45 | 4 10 | 7 15 | .. | 10 30 | .. | 4 10 | .. | 10 30 |
| Bristol ...... | 12 30 | 2 33 | 5.20 | 8 30 | .. | 11 40 | .. | 5 20 | .. | 11 40 |
| Bath ........ | 1 4 | 2 55 | 5 55 | .. | .. | 12 10 | .. | 5 30 | .. | 11 50 |
| Swindon ...... | 2 14 | 3 45 | 7 2 | .. | .. | 1 15 | .. | 7 0 | .. | 1 15 |
| Paddington .. | 5 0 | 5 25 | 10 10 | .. | .. | 4 15 | .. | 10 10 | .. | 4 15 |

#### DOWN TRAINS.

| | ON WEEK DAYS. | | | | | ON SUNDAYS. | | |
|---|---|---|---|---|---|---|---|---|
| FROM | 1 & 2 | | 1 & 2 | Exp. | 1 & 2 | 1 & 2 | 1,2,3. | 1 & 2 | 1 & 2 |
| | p.m. | a. m. | a. m. | a. m. | p. m. | a. m. | a. m. | a. m. | a. m. |
| Paddington .. | 8 55 | .. | 9 50 | .. | 10 15 | 8 55 | .. | .. | .. |
| Swindon ...... | 11 40 | .. | 11 15 | .. | 1 45 | 11 40 | .. | .. | .. |
| Bath ........ | 12 50 | .. | 12 5 | .. | 2 10 | 12 50 | .. | 7 50 | .. |
| Bristol ...... | 1 15 | .. | 7 50 | 12 25 | 2 35 | 1 15 | .. | 7 50 | .. |
| Bridgewater .. | 2 35 | .. | 9 10 | 1 15 | 4 17 | 2 35 | .. | 9 10 | .. |
| Taunton...... | 3 0 | .. | 9 30 | 1 40 | 4 37 | 3 0 | .. | 9 30 | .. |
| Exeter ...... | 4 5 | .. | 10 40 | 2,30 | 4 45 | 5 50 | 4 5 | 7 30 | 10 40 | 6 8 |
| St. Thomas .. | .. | 7 33 | 10 53 | .. | .. | 6 8 | .. | 7 33 | 10 53 | 6 11 |
| Starcross .... | 4 25 | 7 50 | 11 10 | 3 0 | 5 7 | 6 25 | 4 25 | 7 50 | 11 10 | 6 28 |
| Dawlish...... | 4 34 | 8 0 | 11 20 | 3 10 | 5 17 | 6 35 | 4 34 | 8 0 | 11 20 | 6 38 |
| Teignmouth .. | 4 43 | 8 10 | 11 30 | 3 20 | 5 27 | 6 45 | 4 43 | 8 10 | 11 30 | 6 48 |
| Newton ...... | 4 55 | 8 25 | 11 42 | 3.32 | 5 40 | 7 0 | 4 55 | 8 25 | 11 42 | 7 0 |
| Torquay...... | .. | 8 45 | 12 5 | 3 50 | 5 55 | 7 20 | .. | 8 45 | .. | 7 20 |
| Totnes ...... | 5 20 | 9 0 | 12 15 | 4 0 | .. | 7 30 | 5 20 | 9 0 | 12 15 | 7 30 |
| Brent ........ | .. | 9 23 | 12 38 | .. | .. | 7 53 | .. | 9 23 | 12 38 | 7 54 |
| Kingsbridge R | .. | 9 30 | 12 45 | 4 25 | .. | 8 9 | .. | 9 30 | 12 45 | 8 9 |
| Ivybridge .... | 5 50 | 9 39 | 12 53 | .. | .. | 8 9 | 5 50 | 9 36 | 12 53 | 8 9 |
| Plympton .... | 6 7 | 9 55 | 1 8 | .. | .. | 8 25 | 6 7 | 9.55 | 1 8 | 8 25 |
| Plymouth .... | 6 25 | 10 16 | 1 25 | 4 55 | .. | 8 40 | 6 25 | 10 20 | 1 25 | 8 40 |

---

## BRISTOL AND EXETER RAILWAY.
### CONTRACT FOR WORKS.

NOTICE is hereby given, that the Directors of this Company will receive, on FRIDAY the 17th of MARCH, at their Office in Broad Street, Bristol, TENDERS for the execution of the following Works :—

#### CONTRACT No. 3 E.

The formation of the Railway, and the Execution of all Works connected therewith, except the laying of the Permanent Way, of that portion of the line extending southwards from the northern boundary of Field No. 39 (A,) in the Parish of Cullompton, to Chain-stake, 64 Miles 66 Chains, in the Parish of Bradninch, a distance of about 1 Mile 58 Chains.

#### CONTRACT No. 4 E.

The Formation of the Railway, and the Execution of all Works connected therewith, except the Laying of the Permanent Way of that portion of the Line extending southwards from the Chains-stake 66 Miles 39 Chains, in the Parish of Broadclist, to the Southern Boundary of Field No. 69, in the Parish of Silverton, a distance of about 2 Miles 4 Chains.

#### CONTRACT No. 5 E.

The Formation of the Railway, and the Execution of all Works connected therewith, except the Laying of the Permanent Way, of that portion of the Line extending southward from the Chain-stake 69 Miles 48 Chains, in the Parish of Broadclist, to the Boundary-Fence between Fields No. 19 and 20, in the Parish of Stoke Canon, a distance of about 1 Mile 36 Chains.

Notice-posts, showing the commencement and the termination of each Contract, are on the ground.

Drawings and specifications of the above Works will be exhibited at the Engineer's Office, in Temple Meads, Bristol ; and printed forms of Tender may be had at the same office, or at the Company's Office in Broad Street, after MONDAY, the 27th of FEBRUARY.

The Directors do not consider themselves bound to accept the Lowest Tender ; and they expect the Parties to attend at the Office in Broad Street, Bristol, at Twelve o'Clock on the 17th of March.

By Order of the Directors,
J. B. BADHAM, Secretary

Office, 30, Broad Street, Bristol,
17th Feb., 1843.

pumping stations were built between Exeter and Newton Abbot, these being at Exeter itself, Countess Weir, Turf, Starcross, Dawlish, Teignmouth, Bishops Teignton and Newton Abbot. The advantage of greater speed would also enable the South Devon to operate its services on a single line basis and to this end the Company saddled itself with 40 miles of single track. Only 12³/₄ miles, making two sections between Totnes and Rattery, and Hemerdon and Plymouth, gave the opportunity for double line working.

Whilst the good people of Teignmouth welcomed their railway on 30 May 1846, they did not 'benefit' from atmospheric services until 13 September 1847. Delays over costs and construction meant that steam locomotives had the initial 15 months or so on the South Devon. They soon returned again, and whilst the atmospheric working was extended to Newton Abbot on 10 January 1848, the entire project was to be abandoned in September that year having never been implemented beyond Newton Abbot.

Hindsight, of course, showed that atmospheric experiment to have been disastrous, inflicting extensive financial and psychological damage on the company. Shorn of the burden of the atmospheric experiment, the nature of the South Devon line with its fierce curvatures, excessive gradients and circuitous route, gave the line much more of a local character than that of the Bristol and Exeter, offering much in common with the Cornwall and West Cornwall Railways.

Looking at the progress of the two early companies in West Somerset and Devon, the Bristol and Exeter opened to Taunton on 1 July 1842 and in the following year, 1 May 1843, created a temporary terminus at Beam Bridge, ¹/₂ mile east of works on Whiteball Tunnel. This tunnel, ten miles west of Taunton, would mark the final stage of a long climb of some four miles from Wellington – nine miles if one includes the much gentler ascent from Norton Fitzwarren – with gradients of 1 in 90, 1 in 86 and 1 in 80 before plunging into the tunnel for a final stage at 1 in 127. At 1,092 yards, Whiteball Tunnel marked the Somerset-Devon border.

Work was completed on the substantial cuttings and the tunnel itself (driven from 14 vertical shafts) in the Spring of 1844. The remaining section of 22 miles, marking an almost unbroken descent through the Culm Valley to Exeter, originally included three stations, Tiverton Road, later to become Tiverton Junction, Cullompton, and Hele, later known as Hele and Bradninch. Other stations were eventually opened at Burlescombe, Sampford Peverell, Silverton and Stoke Cannon. The Bristol and Exeter opened to traffic throughout on 1 May 1844, an occasion for great celebrations in Devon's historic capital.

In a style that was to be employed on many subsequent occasions the *Exeter Flying Post* spoke of the new line as an "an extraordinary example of Genius over the modest materials by means of ignited coke and boiling water . . . What a field for contemplation is opened up at the thought of what Man has only thus far achieved by the power of steam."

Exeter looked forward to further railway involvement with the development of the South Devon Railway. Incorporated on 4 July 1844, this company experienced, as indicated, more than a fair share of problems. A difficult line to build and to operate it opened in several stages: Exeter - Teignmouth, 30 May 1846, thence Newton Abbot, 31 December that year: Newton Abbot - Totnes, 20 July 1847, Totnes - Laira Green (Plymouth) 5 May 1848: Newton Abbot - Torre, 18 December 1848, and finally, Laira Green to Plymouth, Millbay, 2 April 1849.

If the South Devon Railway was less than inspired in its financial affairs its line was, and remains, endlessly fascinating in engineering and aesthetic terms. The aesthetics and engineering are, indeed, inseparable. In later years, the GWR made much of its coastal route from Exeter to Newton Abbot. The Exe and Teign estuaries presented a distinguished panorama of waterside life, of lush Devon pasture and woodland, and the shifting perspective of distance, light, weather and tide. This, in turn, contrasted with the dramatic spectacle of the sea-wall section from Dawlish Warren to Teignmouth, where the line was carried between cliff-side and sea on what was virtually a causeway, blasted out, embanked and tunnelled.

There were six tunnels along the sea wall. Working westward, they comprised: Kennaway 205 yards, at the western extreme of the beach at Dawlish, then, in rapid succession, Coryton, 227 yards, Phillot, 49 yards, Clerks 58 yards and Parson's Tunnel, 374 yards. East Cliff Tunnel, 320 yards, immediately east of Teignmouth station, was opened out to make a cutting in 1884; the station was rebuilt and the entire layout much improved during the period 1893-1896, a considerable asset to the image of the town as a resort.

A headache to the operating staff, this sea-wall section was a God-send to the late GWR publicity department. Summer sunshine, sand and sea made for the potent mythology of the English seaside holiday; the same sea, transformed by winter wind, was unrelenting.

The early history of the South Devon line provided ample evidence of the sea's destructive power along this exposed section. Two examples of the frequent subsidence from the sandstone cliff formations, and two instances of the extensive damage caused by storms will serve as illustrations. The landslips of February 1853 and August 1885, and the damage from the sea in February 1855 and January 1869 were particularly notable.

Winter gales and prolonged wet weather during early February 1853 resulted in a landslip near the entrance to Holcombe Tunnel at Teignmouth. Passengers and luggage were conveyed by road between Dawlish and Teignmouth, with all local horses and vehicles being requisitioned for that purpose. As the blockage was progressively cleared trains began running up to the site itself with passengers walking across the obstructed section to their waiting trains. The summer of 1885 witnessed another case of subsidence, this time killing and injuring members of an outing at Coryton's Cove, at the foot of the Leigh Mount Pleasure Grounds. 150 tons of earth and rubble fell upon the party of seven, killing two of the servants and one of the children. Another member of the group suffered a broken leg, the remainder escaping with minor cuts and bruising.

Extensive damage to the sea wall west of Parson's Tunnel came with the storm on 16 February 1855. More than thirty yards of the sea wall and embankment were undermined, breached and destroyed by the sea. Again passengers were required to carry their luggage across a temporary bridge. Complete repairs and strengthening were not completed for some time after this. The storm damage of 31 January 1869, was considered to be the worst onslaught yet by the sea. This time, the wall at Dawlish was breached and battered over a distance of

some eighty yards. It was not possible to put in a temporary bridge across this breach until 3 February, because of continued storms. Traffic recommenced on 4 February. The storm was also responsible for destruction of the viaduct outside Penzance station on the West Cornwall Railway. In both cases temporary arrangements kept traffic moving once the danger had passed, and in both cases, the lines were moved slightly inland. Another serious breach, at Rockstone, east of Dawlish, over the winter season of 1872/73 brought further disruption, the most extensive of its kind along the seawall.

West of Newton Abbot there were substantial works but construction and maintenance did not present the repeated problems of the sea wall. The atmospheric system bequeathed the formidable gradients of Dainton, Rattery and Hemerdon Banks. From Aller Junction the line climbed for just over two miles to the first summit at Dainton Tunnel, the fiercest gradient here being a section at 1 in 36. A four mile descent, equally severe at first, brought the line down to Totnes, only to climb away again. Rattery Bank and the long nine mile ascent to Wrangaton then gave way to an easier descent over

seven miles to Hemerdon, where the line fell heavily for two more miles, largely at 1 in 42, to Plympton. From there, relatively favourable gradients brought the line past the temporary terminus at Laira (5 May 1848 – 2 April 1849) to Millbay.

Seven substantial viaducts and Marley Tunnel, 869 yards, together with the severe curvature and gradients carried the line westward into Plymouth, finally opening to Millbay terminus on Monday 2 April 1849. The five timber viaducts on the South Devon line made for definite comparisons with the Cornwall Railway. Like its westerly neighbour, the South Devon's route ran east-west "across the grain"; the valleys and rivers running north-south off the high ground. This meant considerable engineering works. Rattery and Brent viaducts were masonry structures, the former being 201 feet in length and 55 feet in height; the latter, crossing the River Avon, was 171 feet long and 72 feet high. Further west, were the substantial timber works – Glaze, Bittaford, Ivybridge, Blatchford and Slade viaducts – each resting on masonry piers. Glaze Viaduct crossing Glaze Brook was 540 feet long and 81 feet high; Bittaford at 375 feet and 63 feet high, bridged the Lud Brook;

Ivybridge, 756 feet long and 108 feet in height, immediately east of Ivybridge station, crossed the River Erme. On each side of Cornwood Station, Blatchford Viaduct, 885 feet long and 96 feet high, crossed the River Yealm, and Slade Viaduct, 825 feet long and 105 feet high, crossed the River Piall. All these timber viaducts were rebuilt as part of the overall development of the line, reflected in the abolition of the broad gauge of May 1892 and the provision of double-track in the following year.

Doubling had first been pursued eastward from Hemerdon in February 1861, the local press reporting that "double-track had been laid further from the top of the incline." This, presumably, was the section to milepost 238³/₄ from where the line was doubled to Cornwood in May 1893. Cornwood Station was opened in 1852; Wrangaton (renamed Kingsbridge Road, and reverting to its original name in 1895) was the only intermediate station on the Totnes-Plymouth section to open for the initial services in 1848; Ivybridge and Plympton were completed for the official opening of the line to Millbay in 1849 and crossing places were then installed at Wrangaton and Ivybridge, the latter being completed in August 1860.

In covering the opening at Millbay the *Plymouth, Devonport and Stonehouse Herald* recorded:

> We have seldom seen a greater number of persons assembled, they were stationed in every direction whence the line could be seen from Mutley Plain to Millbay.

There were the usual bands, the inevitable bunting, much feasting and prospects of real prosperity and progress. The Mayors of Plymouth and Devonport officiated, the latter believing that the arrival of the railway would "cement the inhabitants of the three towns more strongly." So convinced were they of their prosperous future that they predicted that any system of regional railway communication which was not brought into connection with Plymouth must be deficient. This, of course, was a scarcely disguised swipe at the Devon and Cornwall Central Railway lobby. (See GWR in East Cornwall).

The clearest statement on the significance of the railway for Plymouth focused directly upon prosperity and prestige through the growth of shipping trade. Of the new line it was declared:

> It must tend to the increase of our shipping, as may be fairly expected when the contemplated improvements are carried out in our harbour, both east and west and the railway is actually on the waterside that our exports and imports will be larger; and, in addition, Plymouth will stand a fair chance of obtaining the Packet Station. It will also, we have no doubt, be a port of embarkation and debarkation for passengers on long voyages, and further we may anticipate a larger influx of strangers to visit our neighbourhood, which for the beauty and salubrity cannot be beaten in Great Britain.

It was a confident statement for the future with the tourist potential being recognised, as elsewhere, along the South Devon line. But whilst tourism was acknowledged, and commercial interests made paramount, there were other factors. Together with the celebrations, Plymouth was dealt a considerable blow to its civic pride and to the population generally in the very year that the railway was completed. Cholera attacked the population with the result that, given the excessive death-rate, an official Board of Health investigation was imposed. Robert Rawlinson, reporting for the Board on Plymouth in 1853, wrote:

> It is a lamentable fact and little to the credit of a nation, professing to be in advance of the rest of the world in point of civilisation, that so immense a sacrifice of human life is required before men can be awakened to a sense of the duty which they owe their fellow creatures.

A correspondent to the *Western Morning News* in January 1861 drew attention to related problems, linking railway matters, the docks, and trade, with that of overall image and public perception. His letter was one of complaint and caution, regarding the conditions of the road from Millbay Station to the docks. Sixteen to eighteen steamships regularly discharged and took on passengers each week, with one or more excursions sailing every day in summer and upwards of 100,000 people used the road in the course of a year. He considered the road to be "one of the most public yet worst paved roads in the town," pointing out that, unlike Southampton or Liverpool, there was no appropriate approach road to and from the docks. The story of the actual dock development will be referred to later, but obviously none of these issues or elements ever flourished or declined in isolation.

The arrival of the LSWR in Plymouth in 1876 brought new opportunities to the district and obvious competition for the South Devon/Great Western services. Plymouth North Road opened to traffic on 28 March 1877. The station was built by Order of Parliament at the joint expense of the GWR and LSWR. From May 1876, London South-Western trains began running through Okehampton to their new terminus at Devonport via the GWR (South Devon Railway) broad gauge branch from Lydford to Marsh Mills and, thence into Plymouth over the South Devon Railway main line. The third rail was laid from Lydford southward to give LSWR standard gauge services their access via the Cornwall Junction Loop opened in 1876 to run direct to Devonport. This loop, a masonry viaduct completing a triangular junction immediately west of North Road, also served the interest of the GWR in that through services to and from Cornwall to all points east of Plymouth could run direct into North Road, thus avoiding the time consuming and costly process of reversal at the Millbay terminus.

Although built at what was described as 'joint expense,' 83 per cent of gross receipts for local traffic at North Road went to the GWR as owners of the line. There were also other stipulations in favour of the Great Western. Passengers for LSWR trains were not able to book at either the neighbouring Mutley Station, opened in 1871, or, indeed, at North Road for any destination before Okehampton; no-one was permitted, therefore, to travel in and out of North Road for Lydford, Tavistock, Horrabridge or Marsh Mills, by the LSWR. All LSWR trains stopped at North Road, the first 'up' train also calling at Mutley. Only two 'down' trains stopped at Mutley. Of the Great Western services only the 'Flying Dutchman' and the Mail, morning and night, did not stop at North Road. As indication that North Road had gained an important position, an omnibus service ran between the station and the Royal Hotel and Chubbs whilst the omnibus working between Mutley and Plymouth itself ceased to operate.

Considerable work was required to develop the site at North Road. It was set on an embankment and massive amounts of soil were required to extend the premises. Two main reasons have been given for the fact that the station buildings were very largely of wood. Some sources stress the fact that the LSWR was very anxious to open the station and that construction from wood rather than masonry helped save considerable time, not to mention expense. Another related view was that the embankment restricted the weight of building allowed upon it and that the wooden structure was much less likely to cause subsidence, hence its adoption.

The main entrance was on the south, or 'down' (GWR) side. Here also was the booking office for GWR and LSWR services, refreshment room, bookstall and waiting rooms etc. The platform itself was made of stone, and paved, being 553 feet in length. An overall roof for the 'down' side platform (GWR) covered some 2,549 square yards of the central section; on the 'up' side the roof extended to 2,383 square yards. The two platforms were separated by two through lines set on the original alignment of the South Devon rails of 1849. North Road was modernised and extended in 1908 when two island platforms were added. These were of wood together with the waiting rooms and facilities provided for them. The 'down' (GWR) platform was 750 feet in length; the 'up' being 600 feet. In addition, the 'up' platform was lengthened at the eastern end to reach 790 feet. It was also anticipated that Mutley Tunnel and the two cuttings at each end were to be opened out to provide quadruple track through North Road eastward to Laira. This did not materialise, however and when the LSWR opened its own independent route from Lydford via Tavistock to Devonport and, on again through North Road to its new terminus at Plymouth Friary in 1891, there was yet more pressure put on this vital stretch of double track between Devonport and Laira Junctions.

LSWR services were certainly welcomed within the district when they commenced in 1876. Devonport was particularly forthcoming in its reception. There had been severe complaints and threats on the part of Devonport in the previous decade to reject the South Devon services such was the dissatisfaction with them. As in Cornwall at that time, the community resented the South Devon's monopoly and what was considered its shabby service.

The LSWR and the threat to turn, in the meantime, to shipping, served to indicate this.

Another source of complaint related to the condition of Millbay Station. In something of an understatement the local press wrote that improvements in 1878 gave "a tone to a station which has not hitherto been noted for its beauty or capacity." Millbay, opened in 1849, was extended and partly renovated in 1860, comprising an enlarged arrival platform, a series of new offices for clerks and various officials, waiting rooms and reading rooms for passengers, together with a new first-class waiting room and ladies room for 'down' passengers. With the arrival of the Cornwall Railway from May 1859 considerable extra pressure was put on Millbay's restricted resources, making the improvements of 1860 vital, for as the railway company expressed it, "the prosperity of the railways and of the Great Western Docks goes hand in hand with that of the town at large." 1860 also saw improvements at Plympton Station, the doubling of the line between Plymouth and Devonport, not least, to help with the problem of arrivals and departures at Millbay, and the provision of a third line across Union Street involving the construction of another bridge.

Considerable development followed in early 1878 with much improved waiting rooms, first and second-class dining and refreshment rooms, new staff rooms for telegraph, parcels, cloaks, and for the stationmaster himself. A feature that was given much emphasis was that of the replacement of large amounts of wooden accommodation and fittings with those of masonry and iron. This was particularly so on the arrival platform where the roof was also raised by seven feet and glazed. The verdict from the *Western Daily Mercury* was that "a great deal of taste has been shown, . . . there has been no attempt to be ornate or elaborate."

The timing of this particular rebuilding programme was significant given the developments of the recent past, namely the LSWR at Devonport in 1876 and the Company's own recent scheme in co-operation with the LSWR at North Road, as described above. The local press thought it important enough to note at the time that, 'despite the improvement elsewhere, in other parts of the town, and despite its apparent inconvenient situation, the bulk of the travelling public prefer

Plymouth North Road prior to World War One. A 'Duke' 4-4-0 is seen on an 'up' train in this view westward into the station.

*Cornish Studies Library*

Millbay." It was obviously a time of development driven by changing conditions, not least, at Millbay which had to maintain standards if the Company, and the community itself, was to derive maximum benefit and prestige. To this end, Millbay was entirely rebuilt in 1900, a timely prelude to an outstanding era for the GWR in terms of Ocean Liner services up to the Second World War and for a limited period after it. But here again was a source of competition. The LSWR had established its ocean terminal, opening in 1904 at Stonehouse Pool, reached on a short 1/2 mile branch from Devonport station. Rivalry was considerable until 1911 when under an agreement between the two companies saw an end to the LSWR traffic. A summary of principal services between Plymouth and London by these rival companies in 1909 is given here.

# TRAIN SERVICE BETWEEN NORTH ROAD AND LONDON

## I. GREAT WESTERN RAILWAY

| North Road | Padding- ton | No. of Stops | Av. Speed | Remarks |
|---|---|---|---|---|
| a.m. | p.m. | | m.p.h. | |
| 8.33 | 1.30 | 6 | 45.6 | Breakfast and Luncheon Car Train, via |
| 10.43 | 6.00 | 16 | 33.7 | Westbury, via Bristol and Bath |
| p.m. | | | | |
| *12.32 | 4.45 | 1 | 53.5 | 1st and 3rd Class Luncheon Car via Westbury |
| †12.38 | 6.50 | 8 | | Luncheon Car via Bristol and Bath |
| ‡ 1.45 | 7.05 | 2 | | Luncheon Car via Bristol and Bath |
| 2.10 | 6.45 | 2 | 49.2 | Luncheon and Tea Car, via Westbury |
| 2.20 | 8.30 | 9 | 40.0 | Dining Car, via Bristol and Bath |
| 3.50 | 10.10 | 8 | 38.8 | Corridor Train, via Bristol and Bath |
| a.m. | | | | |
| 8.20 | 3.30 | 12 | 34.9 | Sleeping Car (Sats only) via Weston-super-Mare and Bristol |
| a.m. | | | | |
| 12.15 | 6.45 | 9 | 37.7 | Sleeping Car; except Sat. nights, via Bristol |

| Padding- ton | North Road | | | |
|---|---|---|---|---|
| a.m. | p.m. | | | |
| 5.30 | 12.04 | 9 | 37.5 | via Bath and Bristol |
| 7.30 | 2.11 | 14 | 36.8 | via Bath and Bristol |
| *10.30 | 2.37 | 0 | 54.5 | Luncheon Car, 1st and 3rd Class; longest non-stop run in the world |
| 11.10 | 3.33 | 1 | 51.5 | Luncheon Car to Exeter via Westbury. |
| 11.00 | 3.50 | 2 | | Luncheon Car via Bath and Bristol |
| p.m. | a.m. | | | |
| 9.50 | 4.34 | 8 | 36.5 | 1st Sleeping Car, and 3rd Class, via Bath and Bristol |
| midnight | | | | |
| 12.00 | 6.52 | 9 | 35.8 | Sleeping Car; Monday mornings excepted, via Bath and Bristol |

## II. LONDON AND SOUTH WESTERN RAILWAY

| North Road | Waterloo | No. of Stops | Av. Speed | Remarks |
|---|---|---|---|---|
| a.m. | p.m. | | m.p.h. | |
| 8.33 | 1.47 | 8 | 44.0 | Luncheon Car from Exeter; Corridor Express |
| 10.23 | 3.15 | 4 | 46.9 | Luncheon Car from Exeter; Corridor Express |
| p.m. | | | | |
| 12.18 | 5.47 | 11 | 40.9 | |
| 2.28 | 8.07 | 9 | 40.8 | Luncheon Car from Exeter; Corridor Express |
| 4.11 | 10.34 | 15 | 36.1 | Luncheon Car from Exeter |
| a.m. | | | | |
| 5.09 | 3.35 | 38 | 22.1 | |

| Water- loo | North Road | | | |
|---|---|---|---|---|
| a.m. | a.m. | | m.p.h. | |
| 6.10 | 11.51 | 9 | 40.4 | Breakfast Car to Exeter |
| p.m. | | | | |
| 8.50 | 3.03 | 15 | 37.1 | |
| 10.45 | 3.31 | 3 | 48.2 | Luncheon Car to Exeter; Plymouth Corridor Express |
| p.m. | | | | |
| 1.00 | 6.58 | 11 | 38.5 | Luncheon Car to Exeter |
| 3.30 | 8.28 | 6 | 46.3 | Plymouth Express |
| 5.50 | 11.47 | 15 | 38.8 | Dining Car to Exeter |

* "Cornish Riviera Expresses" via Westbury.
† Winter only.   ‡ Summer only.

A similar vantage point at a later date between the Wars. A platform canopy has been added and the lighting modified.

*Cornish Studies Library*

Torbay took its turn to welcome the railway and all that it promised when the South Devon Company opened its line from Newton to Torquay (Torre) on 18 December 1848. Tourism was to be the definitive traffic; the creation of a prestigious resort being the prevailing factor guiding development. As elsewhere, however, the "Hungry Forties" brought bread riots, cholera and, in 1850, an inspection and report carried out by the Board of Health into the sanitary condition of Torquay. Here, even the best of housing, the villa residences, were subject to criticism for their drainage and sanitary arrangements. Elsewhere in the town there were the usual horrors.

The official opening of the railway began with a distribution of meat and bread to the poor, benefitting up to five thousand people. Press reports recorded that the population turned out "in their best holiday trim" and that despite the temporary recession in trade, particularly affecting the building industry, the town was determined to present its best. The new station, "a handsome and commodious building, principally of wood upon a limestone worked foundation", was sited near the junction of the Paignton and Torquay roads. From here in the early afternoon, a customary 'Special Train' of nine first and fifteen second-class coaches took Directors and local dignitaries to Newton Abbot, the five-mile trip taking 13 minutes. Torquay's optimistic mood and achievement was contrasted with the apparent gloom of neighbouring Newton Abbot. The Special Train and its party spent an hour there before returning, the press noting that "no holiday had infected Newton – the roads were as dirty and the streets as dull as if no pleasure party had been expected." Toasts to Torquay's future also anticipated eager competition with Exeter and Newton Abbot for commerce and trade, the railway being seen as a means of countering the monopoly or centralised nature of prosperity and influence by any one area in particular. Focusing on the tourist potential, one speaker considered Torquay to be "destined to form another metropolis for the West of England," its future being bound with that of the railway:

where nature and art offered their united attractions and which now possessed the only requisite which before was wanting.

With prosperity and progress uppermost, plans were soon tendered for an extension of the railway to Paignton, Kingswear, Dartmouth and Brixham. In the event, it was almost a decade before the Dartmouth and Torbay Railway received the Royal Assent for its line, the Act being granted on 27 July 1857. Prospects of seeing Dartmouth develop as an important trading and Packet port played their part; Paignton had all the potential for tourism, Brixham was an obvious asset in terms of the fish trade, and the line would also open out access to the South Hams, a boon to communications generally and tourism in particular.

Thursday 21 January, 1858, saw the ceremony to cut the first sod; 2 August 1859 marked the opening of the line to Paignton. There were considerable works – twenty bridges, a viaduct and a tunnel – and a steep falling gradient of 1 in 55 from Torquay's original station to the new site at Livermead. The latter was built on rising ground overlooking Torre Abbey Sands to the west of the town. The original Torquay station then became known as Torre, the new site taking the town name. Beyond the station, Livermead Tunnel, 134

yards, took the line under the Paignton-Torquay road and around westward on the coastal section to Paignton at a distance of just over two miles.

Paignton station was described as being "near the beach and rather more than a quarter of a mile from the parish church". The local population here turned out in large numbers to celebrate the occasion. According to the *Torquay and Tor Directory* it was no mean event:

From early dawn the Paigntonians bestirred themselves in making active holiday preparations, business being entirely set aside for the day . . . Flags were hoisted and trees planted in every principal street . . . From all directions by land and by sea thousands of people poured into the streets and were welcomed by merry peels from the parish church bells. . . . The neighbouring towns were deserted by the greater portion of their inhabitants, while the heavily laden excursion trains which arrived from Exeter and Plymouth, and the numerous steamers that plied from equally remote parts indicated the widespread interest which was felt in the proceedings.

The distribution of Paignton's famous plum pudding was also made an important feature of the day. 700 people of Paignton, 150 from Stoke Gabriel and some 300 navvies were given pudding, bread, beef and cider, ample accommodation being provided on Paignton Green, alongside the beach. Paignton's role as a tourist attraction was also given recognition in the directors' proposals to introduce bathing tickets from Torquay to Paignton following similar examples introduced earlier between Exeter and Dawlish.

Further progress for the Dartmouth and Torbay Railway was celebrated on Thursday 14 March 1861 when the line was opened to Brixham Road, later to become Churston. Prior to this, and not forgetting that the new line was still two miles distant from the town itself, Brixham had felt isolated and abandoned. Such was the impact and appeal of the railways:

Before this event they had been shut out from the civilising influences of the outer world and Brixham was known only as a fishing village. It was to be hoped, however, that the railway would affect Brixham as it had done other towns, and that it would be to them as the spear of Ithuriel and make them start into new and vigorous life. . .

Considerable effort was required to bring the line to Brixham Road. Cuttings and embankments abounded, not forgetting two substantial viaducts at Broadsands and Hookhills; Goodrington Marsh consumed vast amounts of material when building the embankment there. The three-mile extension also entailed a stiff climb from Goodrington to Brixham Road, (Churston) this being almost the entire section, at gradients largely unrelenting at 1 in 71 and 1 in 60.

The final section to the terminus at Kingswear opened to traffic on 16 August 1864. This also involved something of a steep descent from Brixham Road for almost 2 1/2 miles to the River Dart, thereafter, running along the riverside on the level into Kingswear itself. A description of the line was given in the *Torquay Directory and South Devon Journal* for 17 August 1864.

Shortly after Brixham Road is passed the line is continued through a deep cutting, and thence on to a high embankment. After another lengthy cutting is passed a second embankment is reached and beyond this is a very beautiful view of the River Dart. Then comes the tunnel (Greenway, 492 yards) through 'trap rock' and 'dry slate' and at this point considerable difficulties presented themselves in consequence of water and clay beds. On leaving the tunnel, the line is carried on Greenway Viaduct which is 500 feet in length, 100 feet high and has ten arches. The viaduct is constructed of substantial masonry. The railway is then laid along the shores of the Dart through Longwood over a timber viaduct which is 40 feet high and resting on quadrupled piles, some of which are 80 feet deep and are driven into the mud below. Beyond Longwood there is a small cutting and soon the Noss Viaduct is reached. This viaduct is 450 feet in length, 35 feet high and rests on quadrupled piles that are 50 feet deep. A cutting is then reached, then there is the floating bridge and the line continues along the shores of the Dart up to Waterhead Creek. The depth of mud here was found to be so great that during thirty days hard material was shot down there to extent of three hundred tons before a foundation could be effected. The line is well constructed; the greatest gradient is 1 in 61 and through Greenway Tunnel, 1 in 100.

Together with the potential for maritime trade, the completion of the line to Kingswear also opened up the South Hams to tourism. This spectacular region of South Devon had much to offer, Kingswear and historic Dartmouth being a more than appropriate gateway to the district. There were also serious plans to extend across the Dart, taking the railway westward to Plymouth, one such scheme being backed by the LSWR to establish standard gauge interests within the district.

To complete this initial survey of the Torbay area and the growth of the railway system there, it remains to be said that the Torbay and Brixham Railway, the two-mile branch from Brixham Road to the terminus overlooking the fishing port itself, opened to passengers on 28 February 1868. The people of Brixham considered the South Devon Railway to have been misguided in the first instance, in not putting the town on the main, through route, leaving it, instead, some two miles distant from Brixham Road. When it did eventually gain improved railway access, in 1868, it was, at best, only to the status of a small branch line. Census returns for Brixham in 1851 reflected a community of 5,936, second only to Torquay within the South Devon district.

The irresistible seaside! Paignton, with the inevitable bathing machines, as photographed in the early years of the century.

*Local Studies Library, Torquay*

Several other branch lines opened during this period were later to play a very useful part in promoting the holiday and tourist image of the GWR. The South Devon and Tavistock Railway, fighting off other rival schemes, opened its route from the junction with the main line at Marsh Mills, three miles east of Plymouth, to Tavistock on 21 June 1859. Regular services began the following day. At just under 13 miles, this was a very heavily engineered line. With heavy gradients of 1 in 60 towards Tavistock the branch included six substantial wooden viaducts on masonry piers, Cann, 127 yards in length and 63 feet in height, Riverford, 127 yards and 97 feet in height, Bickleight, 167 yards and 123 feet in height, Ham Green, 190 yards and 91 feet in height, Magpie, 216 yards and 62 feet in height and Walkham at 367 yards and 132 feet in height. There were also three tunnels – Shaugh 307 yards, Yelverton 641 yards and Grenofen 378 yards. An extension to Launceston, a further nineteen miles, opened on 1 July 1865.

The Tavistock line gave valuable access to Dartmoor, this being improved again with the opening of the Princetown branch across the Moor itself in August 1883. Later developments on these lines by the GWR will be considered later.

Both the Moretonhampstead and South Devon Railway and the Buckfastleigh, Totnes and South Devon lines, likewise, offered access to Dartmoor. The former opened northward from Newton Abbot on 4 July 1866, Bovey and Lustleigh being ideal locations for access to Dartmoor. The Great Western eventually opened the Manor House Hotel at Moretonhampstead. The Buckfastleigh and Ashburton branch running along the Dart Valley from Totnes opened on 1 May 1872, whilst the South Hams district was opened up by the Kingsbridge branch from 19 December 1893.

One of the South Devon's biggest problems with its main line was the extent of single line working. Only the sections, Totnes to Rattery, and Hemerdon to Plymouth were double-track. This was gradually remedied to the extent that by the time the GWR took control in 1876 the bulk of the route had been completed. Newton Abbot to Totnes was first, this being completed in January 1855, making the gruelling climb over Dainton Summit somewhat easier in timetabling terms. Exminster – Starcross followed in September 1860; Exeter St. Thomas – Exminster, June 1861, Exeter St Davids – St Thomas, September 1861, Teignmouth – Newton Abbot October 1865; Starcross – Dawlish February 1874, and Teignmouth to Parson's Tunnel along the sea wall in July 1884. The Dawlish – Parson's Tunnel and Rattery – Hemerdon sections, involving massive engineering and considerable expense, were left to the GWR. In the Torbay district the line from Newton Abbot to Kingkerswell was doubled in the summer of 1876, quadruple track for the Plymouth and Torquay services being in place between Newton Abbot and Aller. Further doubling between Kingkerswell and Torquay was completed by the spring of 1883.

Doubling of the Rattery – Hemerdon section including the task of driving a second bore at Marley Tunnel 869 yards, well underway by 1891, and the rebuilding of the timber viaducts west of Brent, was linked to the abolition of the broad gauge, the latter taking place over the weekend of 21-22 May 1892. Hemerdon to Cornwood was doubled in May 1893; Cornwood to Blatchford Viaduct in November 1893; Blatchford Viaduct to Ivybridge in June 1893; Ivybridge to Wrangaton in August 1893; Wrangaton to Bent, October 1893; Brent to Rattery May 1893.

On the seawall section, doubling between Dawlish and Parson's Tunnel was completed in stages during 1905. Parson's Tunnel to Kennaway Tunnel was opened on 4 June 1905 whilst Kennaway to Dawlish followed on 1 October that year, the sea-wall on this section also being rebuilt at that time.

Abolition of the broad gauge in May 1892 was obviously the end of an era for the Great Western, but it brought urgently needed improvements. The broad gauge block, west of Exeter, prevented any through running of services to other parts of Britain, an advantage enjoyed by the LSWR; also, being in terminal decline, the broad gauge operation could not realistically allow for any innovation in train services, running stock etc – the introduction of corridor services being a case in point. for these reasons the break of gauge at Exeter was an anachronism looking backward to the kind of chaos pilloried by 'Punch' in its cartoons and comments on Gloucester many years before. By the final quarter of the nineteenth century the psychological impact of the broad gauge as well as the mounting practical obstacles made it a liability.

Whilst Exeter until 1892 represented a frontier for the broad gauge, LSWR interests, (as the latter had always intended, in schemes for Devon and Cornwall reaching back to the mid-century) exploited their standard gauge potential for links with other companies, notably the Midland Railway. West of Exeter, and at Plymouth, especially, with the LSWR's own independent line to Devonport, passengers could benefit from through carriage services to various destinations in the Midlands and North, via the Somerset and Dorset system between Templecoombe and Bath. Consider the speech made by the Treasurer of Devonport Corporation welcoming the LSWR to the town in May 1876, when the only access was via the difficult mixed gauge line from Lydford to Marsh Mills, owned by the South Devon/GWR.

> The annoyance hitherto suffered by the break of gauge will be removed and henceforth not only will the town be brought into connection with the narrow gauge system of the country, but your company will have placed the magnificent Government arsenals and works of this district in direct internal communication with the public departments in other parts of the country.

The War Office and Admiralty had long supported the LSWR link to Plymouth "so that stores may go from Portsmouth to Plymouth without break of gauge". Likewise, and less than a year later, in April 1871, Devonport, Plymouth and Exeter Town Councils passed votes of support for the Somerset and Dorset's Evercreech – Bath extension in order to benefit from an "unbroken narrow gauge to the West".

These were evidently more than routine statements on policy towards tourism and trade, they were also clear indications of the LSWR as a determined rival, to use every opportunity to promote its standard gauge line over and against the restrictive broad gauge system of the GWR. Whatever the potential advantages of a broad gauge network in absolute engineering terms it was a concept that, by the 1870s, had been out manoeuvred and superseded; it belonged decisively to the past.

'Castle' No. 5098, *Clifford Castle,* lifts a Plymouth-Liverpool express over the summit of Hemerdon Bank with its formidable sections of 1 in 41 and 1 in 42, 5 July 1955. *R. C. Riley*

*Clun Castle,* No. 7029, at Dawlish with the 'up' *Devonian* on 5 July 1957. No station could have been closer to the sea than this – a considerable boon in summer time but often a nightmare in deepest winter when high tides and on-shore gales wrought havoc. *R. C. Riley*

Under the influence of the LSWR and the Midland Railway in particular, tourism and trade was set to flourish, this being the intention of Ralph Dutton, Chairman of the LSWR in 1876. Through vivid, colourful imagery the Chairman contrasted the industrial districts of the Midlands and the North with the scenic beauty of the West, and in doing so, made an early, interesting appeal to working people.

Everyday they saw evidence of a greater desire on the part of Englishmen to become better acquainted with the beauty of their own land, which formerly they much neglected.

It would be a great advantage to the mechanics of the Midlands and North to be enabled to leave the loom and forge for a while and enjoy this beautiful district. The workman from the ironmills of Staffordshire might leave the rolling of armour plates and come to Devonport and see the completed work floating upon the waters of that magnificent harbour. And the man who sat a the potter's wheel in Staffordshire might leave there the clay and come down to the West to see where that clay was dug.

Considering the programme of improvements by the GWR, the Torquay-Paignton section was doubled in October 1910, but it was not until the summer of 1911 that the benefits of this improvement were apparent. A landslide on the site of the former Livermead Tunnel (now opened out) had blocked the down line almost immediately after the work had been completed. 1911 also saw the lengthening of platforms at Kingskerswell, Torquay and Paignton, and the opening of Preston Platform between the two resorts, the latter being on 24 July. Elsewhere on the main Exeter-Plymouth line, Dawlish Warren, initially known as Warren Platform, was opened on 1 July 1905 with Bittaford Platform, (offering the closest proximity of the main line with the western slopes of Dartmoor) following on 18 November 1907. A new station at Dawlish Warren was provided in 1912, slightly to the north of the original structure, the new site having through roads with long platform loops for the popular tourist traffic to the sea.

The major rebuilding programme in the final years leading up to World War One was that undertaken at Exeter St Davids between 1911 and 1914. Great Western management had also marked out Newton Abbot for complete reconstruction but this had to wait until the inter-war years.

Exeter, the esteemed, ancient cathedral city of the West of England, had always played a vital role in terms of transport and trade. As the gateway to and from the west, St David's station played host not only to a large number of Great Western services covering all manner of destinations, local and national; it also handled all the LSWR traffic to and from North and West Devon, and North Cornwall.

The earliest station, that of the Bristol and Exeter Company dated from May 1844, further development followed with the opening of the South Devon Railway from 1846. Growth of trade and the desire to enhance image and prestige resulted in a new station being opened in July 1864. Two years earlier the LSWR opened their steeply graded link at 1 in 37 from Exeter Queen Street (later Central) down to St Davids, this being just over a half-mile distance. As mentioned earlier, Exeter was, until May 1892, the frontier for broad

EXETER. (N.W.)

Exeter Cathedral's famous West Front, a view which was used extensively in GWR publicity for the cathedral city.

gauge traffic from the West, the transfer point for passengers and freight bound for locations beyond the broad gauge network. This also put pressure on the working arrangements adding considerably to time, effort and costs, helping further to underline the important position of Exeter in terms of the railway network of the West of England. Given the importance of Exeter in railway matters, and as an issue of civic pride, it was necessary that the station itself should always reflect its particular status in the quality and style of its building. The station that emerged in 1864 did not disappoint; nor did its successor, during the rebuilding programme of 1911-1914.

Looking at the 1864 structure, it was described and celebrated both at the time of completion, and almost half a century later, at reconstruction, as one of the finest provincial stations in the Kingdom. The imposing limestone frontage with decorative Bath stone turreting and finials gave it great dignity. An overall roof consisting of a single span was partly glazed with ornamental screens of glass and iron being a feature at each end. This structure gave protection to all five platform faces. On entering the station there were the separate booking offices for the GWR and LSWR services, segregated waiting rooms, refreshment rooms, cloakrooms, telegraph and parcel offices. Immediately beyond these was platform one, the 'down' GWR line to the west, then working across, was the 'up' LSWR line and the island platform. The opposite face was that of the 'down' LSWR line to Plymouth, North Devon and later North Cornwall. Furthest from the main entrance was another island platform, serving the 'up' GWR line for London and Bristol. An ornamental iron footbridge linked these platforms.

Redevelopment, immediately prior to World War One, was essential in view of increased traffic, not least, that linked to the growth of tourism. The station lost its overall roof and the platform layout and running lines were remodelled. Platform one remained the 'down' GWR line, and alongside it was a through road. Next came an island platform serving the 'up' LSWR line and, beyond, the 'down' LSWR. The second island platform served the 'up' GWR main line, and furthest away from the entrance was the 'up' relief line, this island platform being widened considerably at its southern, (Plymouth) end, and later, in the early 1920s, this platform was extended at the northern end. Although the overall roof disappeared to be replaced by individual platform canopy coverings supported by ironwork columns, the original 1864 frontage, described earlier, was retained. The latter was somewhat amended and modernised, with the GWR parentage being carved in stonework during extension work carried out in 1938 and 1939.

The onset of World War in 1914 marked the end of a long almost unbroken period of progress for the railways. It had truly been the age of the railway and for the purposes of the war effort overall, Britain's railways were taken under government control. With the return of peace in 1918 came new conditions soon to become apparent, not least, in the broad structural changes represented by the Railway's Act of 1921, and the Grouping, to form the four great companies. Whilst the inter-war era was no longer the age of the railway and was marked by economic hardship and competition in many areas, there were notable achievements. The growth of the tourist industry was one such case, and here the Great Western Railway played a vital role, encouraging interest in the West Country and making every effort to provide the best possible service for its passengers.

We can now turn to consideration of both these aspects of GWR enterprise, beginning with the Company's considerable record in terms of publicity and image.

'Castle' No. 5069 *Isambard Kingdom Brunel* leaves Exeter St. Davids with the 1.25 p.m. Paddington-Kingswear on 19 July 1958.

*R. C. Riley*

Exeter St. Thomas with 4300 class 2-6-0 No. 6385 on an 'up' stopping service, 3 July 1955. The overall roof from South Devon Railway days looks in good shape in this view southward.

*R. C. Riley*

# Chapter Two
# Railways and Resorts –
# GWR Promotion and Publicity

For the Great Western as for the Southern Railway, Devon was a glittering prize. Both companies became heavily involved in the county, the GWR having no hesitation in declaring it 'Glorious Devon'; 'Shire of Sea Kings', whilst the Southern, likewise, took great pride in its Atlantic Coast association in the north, and in its services to the Channel coast resorts, east of the Exe. Both made it their special business to promote the county's undoubted attractions, and through their respective publicity departments, the railways played a decisive role in shaping Devon's holiday image.

In doing so, they were able to take full advantage of the great variety of landscape and experience that contributed so much to Devon's popular appeal. As a relatively modest post-war promotional work from British Railways put it:

Devon's great charm for holidaymakers is its beauty and its devotion to their entertainment. There are no large factories to mar the perfection of the scenery. Like Cornwall, it has the advantage of a northern and southern coastline of contrasting climate, scenery and interest, where its greatest holiday tours are to be found, but there are also the uplands of Dartmoor, many deep river valleys and delightful villages to be explored; all are within easy reach of the sea.

The genial climate and magnificent landscapes were much apparent, if only to the few, before the arrival of railways in the mid nineteenth century. Torbay, for example, became popular from the time of the French/Napoleonic Wars (1793-1815) when naval officers brought their wives and families to the area, settling them there when Torbay became an anchorage for the Channel Fleet. With Europe closed to those in search of fashionable resorts, landed society, likewise, took advantage, not being disappointed it seems. Teignmouth, Dawlish and Exmouth also benefitted as the reputation of the district grew, setting the style for the rise of prestigious, exclusive watering places. Teignmouth, Dawlish and Torquay reflected the influence of Regency architecture and their respective populations rose steadily in the first thirty years of the nineteenth century.

Considerable growth followed with the arrival of the railway during the 1840s. Rail services to Teignmouth and Dawlish on the South Devon main line began at Whitsun, Saturday 30 May 1846. It was a further two years or so until services from Newton Abbot brought the railway to Torquay.

From the outset, Torquay took all the necessary steps to achieve an exclusive identity. Variously described as "The Capital of the Devon Riviera", "Queen of Devonshire Watering Places", and, "The Italy of England", the essential character and ethos was set. This found clear expression in the writings of Charles Kingsley. Images of peace, harmony and abundance characterised his description of Torquay in 1855:

The rounded hills slope gently to the sea, spotted with squares of emerald grass and rich red fallow fields, and parks full of stately trees. Long lines of tall elms run down to the water's very edge, their boughs unwarped by any blast; here and there apple orchards are bending under their loads of fruit, and narrow strips of water meadow line the glens where the red cattle are already lounging in richest pastures, within ten yards of the rocky pebble beach.

No wonder that such a spot as Torquay with its delicious Italianate climate and endless variety of rich woodland, flowery lawns, fantastic rock-caverns and broad, bright tide-sand sheltered from every wind of heaven except the south-east should have become a favourite resort, not only for invalids but for naturalists.

By the turn of the century, the 1904 volume of *Seaside Watering Places* described Torquay as "the rightful recipient of both Nature and Art, prodigal in their gifts". Almost a decade earlier, another national guide wrote:

Torquay reminds one of a lovely queen of some sunny southern land, who has been transported from her native environment and set down in a far off land . . . There is a harmony of form and a richness of colour about all the neighbourhood, and withal a cleanly and well-groomed appearance about the streets and houses that pleases, while it stops short of any such priggish primness as vexes the spirit of a liberty-loving Briton.

Clear indications of the select, highly fashionable image of Torquay were given in the GWR publication *The Shire of Sea Kings* from 1906. The railway company, no less than the resort itself, was anxious to stress the highly exclusive character and ethos of the resort. Respectability was guaranteed by association:

No one more keenly appreciated the charms of Torquay than the late Queen Victoria who came there as a girl, a young mother, and finally some thirty years ago on a visit to Torquay's most faithful habituee, the late Anne, Duchess of Sutherland.

Edward VII, "a goodly number of Royal personages including the late Emperor of the French and his son" were also included in the veritable 'Who's-Who' at Torquay. Just as importantly, the Great Western was at pains to dismiss any possibility of unseemly association. Atmosphere and character was essential:

Minstrel entertainments and other kinds of beach shows find no favour in the eyes of those who are responsible for the social success of Torquay. On the other hand, yachtsmen, golfers, cricketers and oarsmen find themselves in a place where provision has been made for every kind of sport. Hunting is available, while anglers can choose between lake, river and sea.

The fact that guide books well into the post-war period continued to stress the services of medicinal baths – "Aix and Vichy douches, Navheim vapour and other treatments, light and heat baths, electric baths and reclining baths available for the ordinary composite baths such as sulphur fire and soda etc" – was indicative

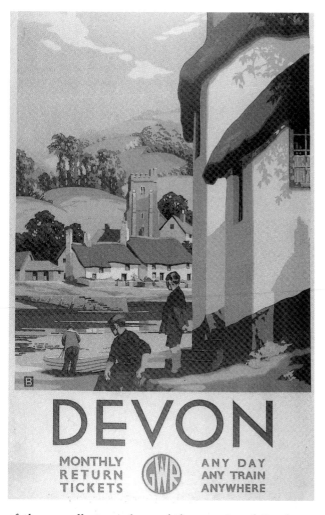

of the overall atmosphere of the resort and its chosen identity.

In the early part of this century, and obviously during the later Victorian period, there was an established etiquette when bathing in the sea. *Ward-Lock* in the closing years of the last century devoted a short section to this essential subject in its guide to Torquay:

Bathing is not carried on promiscuously. It is regulated by well-defined bylaws as in other large seaside resorts. Outdoor bathing may be indulged in at the following points:

**Ladies** – At Tor Abbey Sands, at the north-east side of Corbyn's Head; at the ladies bathing cove adjoining the Bath Saloons, and at Meadfoot.

**Gentlemen** – At Livermead, near the west side of Corbyn's Head; at Peaked Tor, between the Imperial Hotel and Lands End, and at Meadfoot.

At Corbyn's Head and Meadfoot there are machines and at Peaked Tor there are dressing rooms where attendants provide towels and costumes for a small charge. Good bathing may also be had at Babbacombe and Anstey's Cove.

S P Mais in his now famous GWR publication *Glorious Devon* presented the reader with a veritable panorama; a perspective of sights, senses and colours, definitive of Torquay's unique character. His work in this instance must have been particularly well received by the resort itself and by the railway company serving it. The heavily 'feminine' charms of the resort are offered us here in a celebration of detail and delight:

Torquay unveils her beauties very gradually. It is not from the railway which is tucked away unobtrusively, that her particular glories are to be seen. Built like Bath and Rome on seven hills, her full majesty is not to be realised unless perhaps from the sea or from the height of her new reservoir. Each separate arc of beauty is self-contained and individual. Visitors may arrive in their tens of thousands, but within a few minutes of their arrival they become invisible. Here is no hard glittering ruler-line of a grand promenade, going endlessly, tirelessly on until it emerges into the grander, no less straight and tiring promenade of the next resort. Instead, you find yourself in the cleft of a vast bay, where you may see without being seen. The high rocks stretching down to the front are hidden in a forest of wonderful exotic palms and flowers which seem to flourish nowhere but here.

Among these you wander along myriad labyrinthine paths looking out over the exquisitely-shaped bay from red-roofed Paignton to the distant masts of trawlers nestling under their green headland.

The sea wall, separating the promenade from the splendid stretch of Torre Abbey Sands is made of red 'conglomerate', a warm rugged and most picturesque compound of sandstone.

Waldon Hill, with white sunny houses in every nook stands between you and the town, but you have the alternative of encircling its base either through the Princess Gardens by the side of the jetties of the outer harbour, or along the terrace gardens among the cacti and the palms, where honest English honeysuckle, bramble, and nasturtium mingle with aloes and rare hothouse lilies.

The inner and outer harbours are always full of interest with racing yachts, excursion steamers, motor boats, cargo steamers and fishing smacks and ocean going tramps, and as an occasional treat gunboats, mine-sweepers or a cruiser . . .

Beyond the swimming baths there is a climb to a high level limestone plateau known as Daddy Hole Plain, from which there is a fine view of Shag Rock at our feet, far below, and the strange arch jutting out from the mainland, known as London Bridge. Berry Head lies four miles out across the bay, and immediately in front of us on our coastal journey lie the shining white sands of Meadfoot in their setting of the green trees of Lincombe Hill. Beyond this is the famous broad Marine Ilsham Drive, so cunningly built that even in this tree-covered hilly area the tourist can realise something of the changing colours and contours of the peninsula of Hope's Nose. There are rocks out at sea, one white with gulls, the other black with cormorants. There is Hope Cove with its myriad rocks inviting scramblers to descend from Black Head, and a hundred shady walks to Anstey's Cove, a sandy bathing bay bounded by giant limestone rocks, completely embowered among the trees. Near the top of this cove is Kent's Cavern, by far the most historically interesting feature of Torquay.

Beyond Anstey's Cove is Redgate Beach, after which we climb Wall's Hill to be richly rewarded by looking down on Babbacombe and Oddicombe.

Babbacombe Beach contains a few thatched whitewashed cottages clinging to the steep wooded hillside, and a tiny jetty. Oddicombe Beach is separated from it by a series of loose boulders, and is a wide strip of pebbles flanked by red sandstone cliffs with woods and rich green fields stretching to the cliff edge.

Even in the Torquay area there is no view to compare with that to be had from the top of Babbacombe Down on a clear day. The whole sweep of that fine bay that ends in Portland Bill can be seen, and through glasses one can pick out from the red and white cliffs all the East Devon watering places from Lyme Regis to Exmouth. Nearer and clearer are red Dawlish, red Teignmouth, and the perfect blend of clear blue sea, red sandstone, green field and silver yellow sand that make up the incomparable charm of Oddicombe, Petitor and Watcombe Glen, least known of all Torquay's hidden arbours.

Whilst S P Mais celebrated this landscape for the GWR and readers of *Glorious Devon,* the local corporation took decisive action to conserve it for posterity. In April 1929, for example, Torquay marked the purchase of the coastal stretch from Maidencombe to Labrador. At much the same time a new Palm House was opened to the public in the grounds of Torre Abbey.

Torquay Corporation worked in conjunction with the GWR to great effect. Both were seen to actively promote the resort, as in this, one of numerous occasions, the 'Gala Week' in June 1923. Arranged by the corporation to advertise Torquay, this event was well supported by the Great Western. Journalists, railway officials and invited guests travelled from Paddington in special coaches added to the Torbay Limited express. The Gala included a water carnival, sports, steamer trips on the River Dart and the opportunity to inspect and admire the new Marine Drive under development to link the station with the town. The station was extensively decorated, identifying closely with the festivities. During its centenary year the Great Western was pleased to announce further developments at the resort. Describing the initiative as being "of the usual generous proportions" the GWR Magazine recorded Torquay's purchase of Cockington Court "with 270 acres of land in the adjoining village". The cost was £50,000, with a further £23,000 being spent on buying 2½ miles of coastline which then linked Torquay town boundary with that of Teignmouth.

TORQUAY
THE RIVIERA OF DEVON

Illustrated handbook free from
CORPORATION PUBLICITY MANAGER
30, Marine Spa Offices, Torquay

In keeping with the character of a distinguished resort the Great Western Railway had earlier provided Torquay with a new station. This replaced an earlier less satisfactory structure dating from the time of the extension from Torre to Paignton in 1859. Occupying the rising ground near Chelston, overlooking the Torre Abbey Sands and commanding an extensive view of the town and Torbay, this site became the principal station for the resort. This caused considerable controversy when the original station, of 1848, renamed Torre in 1859, lost its pre-eminent status. The new station opened in September 1878, making its contribution to the positive image of the resort generally.

The local press in the form of the *Torquay Directory* provided a detailed description of the new facilities early in 1878:

The construction of the New Railway Station at Torquay is progressing satisfactorily . . . The station on the up-line will be 244 feet in length, and one storey in height; there will be two waiting rooms; a boiler house for supplying hot water tins for passengers and apartments devoted to various uses.

The down station will be of the same length as the up, but the platform extends fifty feet further in the direction of Torre and is covered so as to protect passengers from the weather. The refreshment room is on the down side . . . There are cloakrooms, lavatories, parcel office, telegraph office, also waiting rooms and a variety of offices for the convenience of passengers and for those employed at the station. Access is gained to and from the up and down platforms either by the carriage road, or by the ornamental footbridge which connects the two stations at the Levermead end.

The walls are of black marble, brought form Pomphlete, with Doulting stone dressings. The roofs of the platforms are supported by cast iron columns; latticed girders rest on the columns and to these girders ornamental cast-iron cantilevers are fixed and these support the timbers of the roof. The roof projects so as to cover the entire platform; passengers will therefore be able to enter or leave the carriages under shelter.

On the approach side of both platforms there will be a verandah, under which carriages will be able to drive up to the entrance. The work is being most substantially carried out by the contractors Messrs Vernon and Ewings, of Cheltenham, on behalf of the Great Western Railway Company.

More evidence of the appeal of Torbay and the vital role of the railway to tourism. Passengers packing the 'up' platform at Torquay watch away the 8.40 a.m. Paignton-Nottingham on 23 August, 1958. Once again, the contrast between 'up' and 'down' platforms is all too apparent. The departure train was headed by a 'Hall' and banked by 5700 Class No. 5796.          *P. Gray*

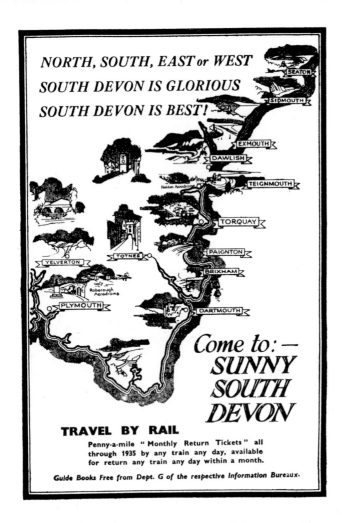

In 1910 the railway line was doubled to Paignton, indicating the increased traffic to the resort. Paignton, well known as a 'family resort', was praised for its magnificent beaches. Both the GWR publications *The Shire of Sea Kings*, and the better known *Glorious Devon*, drew attention to Paignton's superb beaches, but gave very little time to the resort. *Glorious Devon* recognised the merits of the parish church and noted that there was an old picturesque harbour at the west end of the town. Other than this, and a reference to Paignton's famous white-pot pudding, there was this somewhat bland statement:

> For those who like on holiday a continuous round of tennis, golf, bathing and yachting, Paignton is much to be recommended. It is bracing, and owing to its comparative freedom from trees and absence of hills, gets all the sun that shines.

Paignton did a great deal to attract visitors during the inter-war years. Building on its family image and its reputation for excellent beaches and bathing, the Goodrington Park and related developments – gardens, boating lakes, promenade, cafes and car parks costing some £75,000 – did much to enhance the resort. Sir Robert Horne, Chairman of the Great Western Railway, visited Paignton on 23 May 1936 to officially open the new municipal park and related improvements. The Chairman of Paignton Urban Council described the project as "a significant milestone in Paignton's phenomenal success":

> Encouraged by past developments they had transformed what had been an unsavoury swamp

into a healthy delightful open space and were planning further improvements.

The Chairman of the GWR referring to Paignton that day as "a fairer paradise than ever before", likewise praised the council's initiative:

> Having been achieved by the imagination, courage and spirit of the men who had guided the affairs of the town (they) by the creation of these great promenades had saved the land from the ravages of the sea and redeemed a drab and distressing marsh to convert it into a beautiful park.

Extensive development of the sea-front area from Preston Sands to Goodrington was completed during the thirties and further acquisition of land, at Broadsands waited on the return of peace to make yet more valuable post-war attractions.

*Holiday Haunts*, in 1947, stressed the attractions of Paignton as the family resort:

> It is run on modern lines with fine hotels on the sea-front, spacious promenades laid out with lawns and flower beds and long stretches of sands on which there are rows of bathing huts and tents. Extensive pleasure grounds, yacht ponds, Peter Pan playground and a zoo were also offered with a regatta and a carnival contributing to a full programme of amusements.

*Holiday Haunts*, 1959, portrayed Paignton in the superlative, as the all-round family resort. In an extensive entry celebrating the attractions, 'Holiday Haunts' also conveyed the full vigour and variety of

Busy times at Paignton in early September 1954. Road traffic is at a halt and pedestrians watch the trains at the level crossing as 'Hall' No. 5949, *Trematon Hall* enters the station with the 6.40 a.m. Leicester-Paignton, passing 'Grange' No. 6821, *Leaton Grange*, heading the 2.45 p.m. Paignton-Paddington.

*P. Gray*

holiday time at Paignton emphasising its popular appeal and the commitment of the town to growth and success. The images were those of vitality and studied progressive service, marking out, and best expressing a style of tourism that, owing almost everything in character and achievement to the inter-war years, was also approaching a watershed. Shifts in image and style during the sixties visited considerable change, welcome or otherwise, upon tourism and transport alike. For these reasons, 1959 might be taken as a significant year, resonant of past and present, of comparison, continuity and change.

Paignton is a modern resort in the centre of beautiful Torbay . . . The main part of the town is on a level site, a great consideration for those who dislike hills, and the magnificent esplanades which run for nearly three miles are exceptionally spacious. Paignton makes every possible provision for sport and amusement, with fine hotels along the sea-front, promenades laid out with lawns and flower beds and long stretches of sand on which there are rows of bathing huts. Preston Green, a pleasure ground of about 10 acres affords ample space for playing games. A short cliff-walk past the harbour leads to the splendid Goodrington Sands. Paignton not only has miles of gently sloping sandy beaches offering safe bathing and paddling, but cliff-gardens, promenades, seaside cabins and huts, up-to-date bathing stations, putting greens, a large boating lake, model yacht sailing ponds, a Peter Pan playground, attractive cafes and tea gardens and beautifully laid-out flower and rose gardens and shrubberies. The sands at Broadsands beyond Goodrington (where the GWR opened an excursion platform for one year from July 1928) are now very popular, and the mansion of "Oldway", a former residence of the Singer family, modelled on the Palace of Versailles, has become the civic, social and recreational centre of Paignton. The beautiful grounds cover 20 acres and tennis, bowls and putting may be enjoyed. There is also a cafe and tea gardens. Paignton has a full programme of amusements during the season ranging from a regatta in August, athletic meetings, aquatic galas, bowling and tennis tournaments, veteran car rallies and horse-jumping to concerts and carnivals.

Activity on and off the rails at Churston on 7 July 1956. 1400 Class 0-4-2T No. 1472 waits in the bay with the auto-trailer on the Brixham service whilst two long-distance holiday trains occupy the up and down platforms. 'Hall' Class 4-6-0 No. 4973, *Sweeney Hall*, waits with the 3.20 p.m. Kingswear-Cardiff, crossing with 'Castle' Class No. 4082, *Windsor Castle,* on the 10.20 a.m. Paddington-Kingswear. Note also the now vintage road transport in the shape of the Morris Commercial Post Office van on the platform and the motor coach, awaiting passengers for the Brixham holiday camps.                                                *P. Gray*

'Castle' No. 4098, *Kidwelly Castle* with the Kingswear portion of the *Royal Duchy* passes Waterside caravan site on 27 June, 1961. Torbay forms a magnificent backdrop for this study of holiday imagery and the railway in the West Country landscape.          *P. Gray*

Kingswear in the summer of 1946. 'Star' Class 4-6-0 No. 4026 backs out of the station with the empty stock from its Exeter stopping service on 6 July 1946. The terminus had been extensively redeveloped during 1928-29 and this locomotive too had been somewhat modified at that time. Originally named *King Richard*, No. 4026 was renamed *Japanese Monarch* in 1927, this name being removed in 1941.                    *Pursey Short*

Beyond modern Paignton one soon encountered the more traditional delights of Brixham, a fishing port after the style of Newlyn or Port Isaac. S P Mais, perhaps with Paignton in mind, drew inevitable comparisons. Describing Brixham as made for business rather than pleasure, Mais considered the port to be "far more aesthetically satisfying than any of the resorts built to attract the merely leisured":

In the first place it is grey and old. Its streets are narrow, and connected by long flights of steps quite different from, but just as attractive and individual as the cobbled streets of Clovelly. Then one is struck by the size, solidity and beauty of the outer harbour, which is always full of red-sailed, black trawlers with their splashes of yellow and red paint on every spare bit of woodwork.

Dartmouth was the subject of unreserved praise by the Great Western writers. Its magnificent setting, undeniable charm and its extensive historical associations gave it a quintessentially English character.

The writer of *Glorious Devon* saw it in highly romantic terms offering up an idyllic, impressionistic response full of atmosphere and, appropriately, considered from the window of a Great Western carriage as the train drew ever nearer to Dartmouth, by the water's edge:

To reach it you merely take a train to Kingswear and cross by ferry to Dartmouth. There are few sights to compare with that first view across the water. If you chance upon it by night you get a vision of a deep, broad black water winding its way inland through steep valleys, thronged with trees to the very edge of the lapping waves. Green, white and red lights tossing in midstream betray the presence of white-sailed yachts and ocean-going liners, barges and yawls at anchor. The lights on the opposite hill dotted about so

precipitously that it is none too easy to tell where the houses end and the stars begin, give the impression of a nocturnal pageant in a fairy castle, an impression that is only heightened as one is drawn quietly across the Dart, a river that requires but little imagination to interpret as the moat that separates the enchanted citadel from the mundane world.

Once inside this veritable 'enchanted citadel' the reader of *The Shire of Sea Kings* is soon invited to consider the delights of a walk to the open sea. Once again, it was an excursion into the senses, emphasising the colour, sights, sounds, and smells of a classic English landscape:

. . . the narrow streets running between the houses giving glimpses of water, of old bastions and towers, of gardens hanging on steep slopes, of fuchsias and pelargoniums running riot in the warm, damp air, of red rock and green foliage jumbled together in the wildest of tangles, of blue, still water below, with gulls, living foam-flakes, swaying, chattering over the surface.

In the opposite direction, *The Homeland Handbook* enthused over the trip up-stream by steamer to Totnes, this being, by common consent, the 'only' way to visit the historic town, compared favourably with the much larger city of Chester, and marking the highest navigable reaches of the River Dart. Totnes offered a Norman castle, distinguished architecture from the time that it comprised one of the smallest walled towns in England, an ancient Guildhall and narrow streets characteristic of the Middle Ages, when the town first received its charter.

In linking both Dartmouth and Totnes, the *Homeland Handbook* asked of the River Dart: "What stream is there so typically English, so intensely Devonian?":

Steamer Quay at Totnes, from where one could embark on an outstanding river trip to Dartmouth and the sea, enjoying the spectacle of "England's Rhine". Elsewhere the River Dart was described as "typically English" and "intensely Devonian."

It sweeps along in leisurely fashion, here broadening out into a veritable lake and sparing some water to an inlet running far inland, left or right, and at another point becoming narrow. But narrow or broad it is hedged in with hills crowned with trees that creep down to the water's edge and cluster so closely that the actual hills are seldom to be seen; there is only a succession of densely foliaged trees – hanging woods mirrored in the stream – with here and there the chimney of a mansion rearing its head among the greenery, and at several points, villages snugly ensconced in some leafy valley ...

Beyond all question, the way to extract the most pleasure from the Dart is to drift with the tide in the glow of a summer evening, when the sunlight slants across the stream, turning the reaches into golden lakes, and when the dense shadows of gigantic oaks that bend over it, contrast with the branches far above.

Dartmoor, the wild and romantic moorland expanse, the last wilderness of Southern England, was obviously in great contrast to the lush pastoral image of Devon. With the growth of tourism in the later nineteenth century, and the fashion for organised walking tours and rambling in the twenties and thirties, the great discovery of the English countryside went ahead, Dartmoor rapidly became a priority. Long before the widespread appearance of the motor car, however, it was always the railways that brought the visitor to Devon, and the railways, working with local road transport, that offered access to the remote, but eminently desirable landscapes of the Moor.

The Great Western and the Southern Railway offered various approaches to the delights of Dartmoor. From the south, the Great Western's branch line from Newton Abbot to Mortonhampstead provided relatively easy access both from the terminus itself with its Great Western Railway Manor Hotel and, especially, from Bovey Tracy. Ashburton, the terminus of the beautiful Dart Valley line from historic Totnes, also gave its passengers the opportunity to visit Buckfast Abbey en route. This line from Totnes northward to Buckfastleigh has been preserved allowing us all the opportunity to savour the atmosphere of a Great Western branch line in one of Britain's most desirable landscapes. Further westward, on the GWR mainline to Plymouth, the smaller local stations at Wrangaton, Bittaford Platform, then Ivybridge and Cornwood, provided gateways to the southern limits of the Moor, Bittaford giving closest proximity.

In the far west, the GWR's Launceston branch through Yelverton, Tavistock and Lydford gave access to the western reaches of the Moor. The further branch from Yelverton through Dousland to Princetown itself took its passengers across the Moor, winding and climbing its lonely, wonderful way into the wilderness. The Southern Railway route from Exeter to Plymouth, likewise, gave direct access from its main line stations at Okehampton, Lydford and Tavistock. Okehampton gave the opportunity to strike into the northern limits of Dartmoor, the line, from that point to Tavistock, running along the northern and western fringes of these high lands.

Never merely a visit, Dartmoor was an experience. It has always needed to be seen in its various moods – the Tors on bright sunlit days, of infinite clarity across an ancient but benign landscape, chorused by skylarks in the purest of air. But there would always be the dark days, with rain and lowering dense cloud, betokening doom and thoughts of sanctuary by a warm fireplace, the refuge from a brooding indeterminate melancholy. Or, again, there were the surprises, as one discovered remote communities, such as Manaton, high up in the Moor, but offering much of the atmosphere of an English country village, the kind found far from its moorland location. Becky Falls, not far from Manaton (included here, later, as one of the GWR's outings from its books of rambles), showed that the great variety of Dartmoor was by no means an unrelenting, awesome landscape.

As the northern terminus of the branch from Totnes, Ashburton was very much a gateway to Dartmoor and a thriving local market town. The distinctive overall roof, a feature of several GWR branch lines in Somerset and Devon, was provided when the line opened to Ashburton on 1 May, 1872. This station has had the distinction of being twice opened and twice closed to passengers. The first occasion came with the entire branch in November 1958, thereafter, the line was re-opened privately in April 1969 but the upper section, between Buckfastleigh and Ashburton, was closed from April 1971 in connection with heavy improvements to the A38 road and conversion to dual carriageway, incorporating the former railway alignment along the valley. No. 1427 was photographed at the terminus on 11 October 1958.

*P. Gray*

31

# MANOR HOUSE HOTEL

## MORETONHAMPSTEAD (Devon)
### (Under the Management of the Great Western Railway)

18-HOLE
GOLF COURSE
IN
HOTEL GROUNDS

This hotel is ideally situated on the edge of Dartmoor, 700 feet above sea-level, and has its own grounds of 200 acres of park and pleasure lands. Central heating and electric lighting are installed throughout the building, and the drainage and water supply are of modern type.

The hotel, fully licensed, is being considerably enlarged during the winter 1934-5. The alterations are expected to be complete by the end of April and will provide the visitor with the latest comfort known to hotel science. Hot and cold water will be laid on in every room and many additional private bathrooms will be provided. Golfers will find in the Golfers' " corner " ladies and gentlemen's changing rooms with private lockers, drying rooms, etc., attached ; a new departure in modern comfort. Squash Racket Court, Recreation Room and facilities for playing Badminton are also being provided.

Trout-fishing in the River Bovey on the estate and Trout and Salmon fishing in the River Teign. Tennis on hard and grass courts, croquet, bathing pool. A very fine 18-hole golf course (5,571 yds.) has been constructed in the hotel grounds.

Winter terms : 4½, 5½, 6 and 7 guineas per week, including meals, accommodation, baths, early morning and afternoon teas. Garage accommodation for 20 cars, including 10 lock-up garages. Nearest station Moretonhampstead (2 miles). Hotel Bus meets principal trains.

Illustrated Brochure obtainable from Hotel Manager or Mr. G. J. Walker, Great Western Royal Hotel, Paddington Station, London, W.2.

*Telegrams :* " Manorotel, North Bovey."     *'Phone :* Moretonhampstead 55.

---

The *Homeland Handbook* wrote of Manaton as:

. . . a typical English village. There is the green surrounded with trees, where the geese are feeding, the thatched cottages, the church under the hill, and near is Church House where you may lodge under a roof that has sheltered many celebrities; but the rugged rocks of Manaton Tor, just behind the church, give it an unmistakable local character. Each tor on the Moor has its own distinguishing feature. Manaton flaunts from every cranny banners of holly and mountain ash,

glorious in autumn with glowing berries.

Hay Tor, to the west of Bovey Tracey, was popular because of its accessibility. S P Mais considered a visit to this landmark from the railway at nearby Bovey, to be no more than "nibbling on the fringes", even if it was, inevitably, the most popular 'nibble'.

*The Homeland Handbook* at the turn of the century told its readers of the reward awaiting them at the tor:

No one has seen Hay Tor who has not climbed the rock; there are steps cut and a railing put by them.

Now you can see the low mountain range of Dartmoor Forest rolling away before you, belt upon belt of undulating tableland. In the valley below her Widdecombe-in-the-Moor, with Hamildon behind it. Down this valley a belt of fertility fills the hollow to Leasdon; on the left beyond it are the woods of Holne Chase, Buckland Drives with Buckland Beacon. The conical hill conspicuous in the south is Brent Beacon. Ugborough Beacon stands beyond again, with Three Barrow Tor. Far away to the right, on the north is Gausand Beacon, which used to dispute height with dim Yes Tor, near it.

Looking close at hand we see every ridge is topped with rock or 'tor' of more or less importance. Hunter Tor, on the right is a group of rocks; Hound Tor can be singled out from the wild clatter on the hillside. They recall the legends of the "Wild Huntsman and the Whisht Hounds" who howl and hunt the Moor on winter nights, the Whisht hounds being the souls of unbaptised babies.

To the *Homeland Handbook,* it was impossible to vulgarise Dartmoor. Once out on the Moor:

Humanity is as much belittled as the animals: picnic parties and excursionists come up to Hay Tor, and are lost to view among the boulders: their laughter and chatter rings as harmlessly in the air as the bird cries.

For those unable to walk long distances there was always the rail journey from Yelverton up to Princetown. S P Mais considered that "from the point of view of scenic effects there is no railway journey in Britain to compare with that between Plymouth and Princetown. *Holiday Haunts* called it "a branch railway which climbs the wild hills like a goat".

Manaton, a moorland location near Lustleigh on the Moretonhampstead branch. This delightful village was described as 'typically English' and was particularly lush and green, pastoral in character despite its position.

*Author*

32

*Ramble No. 8.*

# BRIMLEY, HAYTOR ROCKS, BECKA FALLS, LUSTLEIGH CLEAVE AND VILLAGE AND BOVEY TRACEY.

### (4½, 6, 8½ or 13 miles.)

This ramble includes a number of well-known beauty spots, but it will no doubt be realised that the beauty along the delightful route chosen is probably greater than that at the actual beauty spots and that, to paraphrase R. L. Stevenson, it is better to travel pleasurably than to attain.

If a cheap day ticket is taken for the rail journey, it will be necessary to book to Bovey, as these tickets are not issued to Brimley Halt, at which it is advisable to alight, as this will save a detour and improve the walk. In this case, turn left over the bridge at the top of the approach path and bear right at the first fork, ignoring then all side turnings and signposts. Continue through Lower Brimley and just beyond a wayside pump at Upper Brimley, a little over a mile from the Halt, take a right forward path up from a gate standing back from the road. Cross the fields, taking an opportunity of looking back to admire the view at the top of the rise ; then bear very slightly left down to a stile admitting to a lane, where turn right.

Take the second left turning in less than a mile and just beyond Middlecott Farm follow a due west indistinct path from a gate on the right, keeping up to a stile under some trees and continuing to a lane right of a farm. This is known as Iron Mine Lane and should be followed forward through an exquisite bit of woodland, with a small stream rushing down, first on the left and then on the right. Just beyond a wooden fence near the top, take a left path up a few steps and between some upright iron bars, bearing right with the path to a road. There is an inn to the left for refreshment, if required, or another opportunity by going up the forward road and turning right later to the moor, when Haytor Tea House will soon be found on the left, three miles from Brimley Halt.

Having refreshed, follow any of the paths up to Haytor Rocks, the scaling of which is assisted by an iron rail from about halfway up and some steps cut in the rock, which has been worn very smooth by the numerous climbers. This eminence of nearly 1,500 feet is one of the finest view-points in Devon and commands extensive views over Dartmoor on one side and across the wide valley to the sea beyond Teignmouth on the other. Some idea of the immense stretch of beautiful countryside included in the panorama can be gathered from the number of points on these rambles from which Haytor has already been mentioned as a distant landmark.

Unless going west towards Widecombe-in-the-Moor to connect with No. 9 Ramble, a northerly direction must be taken on leaving, somewhat leftward from the steps, passing left of the old quarries and over the left shoulder or the top of Black Hill, the highest point on the way. Paths can be taken, but as there are a number of them care must be taken that they do not mislead from the right direction.

Beyond Black Hill bear right and follow the direction of the hedge below to the road near its junction with a leftward moorland road. Turn left here on the tarred road and descend for a good half mile, looking out for a gate on the right just before reaching the river bridge. Follow the path from this, bearing left in the road, in which turn right and veer somewhat left on a path running past the refreshment hut. This will lead down to Becky Falls, as they are popularly called, though the real name is Becka, after the Becka River, of which they are part. Some disappointment may be felt over the falls, as, though the rock formation is fine, they are not what they were, some of the water having been diverted for commercial purposes.

Those who wish to finish at the six-mile stage can get a 'bus from here to Bovey Tracey, but to continue for the most beautiful part of the walk cross the river by the numerous rocks and climb up slightly leftward to the main path, where turn right. Drop with the path and rise somewhat leftward, keeping up near the hedge, but

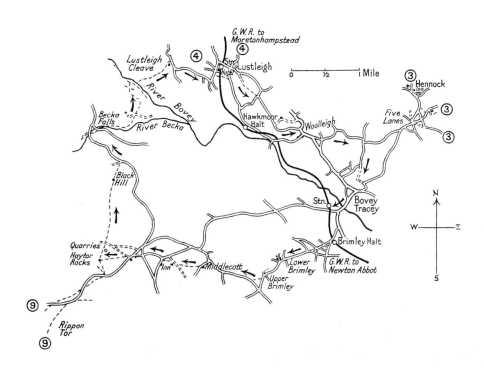

not going through it. This is one of those paths that are in danger of being lost through insufficient use, as, though it is a perfectly good path, the bracken and brambles grow so luxuriously that they are liable to choke it unless there is plenty of passage through, often with the vigorous use of a stick.

On joining a cart track, follow it upward, but leave it almost immediately for a right forward path coming out later into the open, with a splendid view over both river valleys. Continue round leftward near the hedge and descend, Lustleigh Cleave being seen ahead at first. Bear left with the path for nearly half a mile, then follow it down to the right, soon passing between two left forward stone gate-posts and bearing right to the River Bovey, which follow rightward to a wooden bridge.

Cross this and take the main path from it up through the famous Lustleigh Cleave, bearing right and later left on nearing a hedge, which follow upward, with the group of rocks in various fantastic shapes on the left, and then down to a gate. Just before this, there is the gate of a refreshment cottage for tea; or this can be obtained in Lustleigh in half a mile by passing through the gate below and on into the road, where turn right and take the first left fork, avoiding further turnings or paths. Soon after passing a fork on the right and a chapel on the left, turn left into Lustleigh, a very charming village, full of camera studies and picturesque corners, 5½ miles from Haytor Tea House.

Tea can be obtained at the little shop just before the smithy, or at the Cleave Hotel to the right from the church and those who wish to finish here after 8½ miles can reach the station by the left path just beyond the hotel, taking a single ticket to Bovey for 5d., if a cheap day ticket to that station was used on the outward journey.

To continue the walk, turn down to a right-hand corner from the church, or left if coming from the hotel, pass a quaint little stone aqueduct, go under the railway and take a left forward path by another little stream to a house with an interesting old porch, dated 1680. Keep round to the left from here and follow the road to a cross road, where turn right, ignore any turnings and continue later up an enclosed stony path and straight through a delightful wood to a road. Here avoid the immediate right and left turnings and take the right forward lane, pass a left and subsequent right turning lower down and proceed up and leftward to the main road, where turn right through part of Woolleigh till a forward lane leads off to the left.

A mile can be saved here if desired by following the main road into Bovey Tracey, but those who do not object to a detour and a climb will find it well worth while to take the forward lane, crossing a transverse one shortly and bearing right at a drive gate up a green lane between the mossy banks of a beautiful wood.

At the cross roads at the top, there is an opportunity for connecting with No. 3 Ramble by taking the forward road for nearly a mile, mainly along a ridge with fine views, to a junction of ways called Five Lanes. Here, the left of two forward lanes will lead to Hennock, a hilltop village with a prospect; or the right forward lane can be taken almost direct to Trusham Station, about 1½ miles from Five Lanes. A mainly footpath alternative to that station is also available by going through the farmyard just beyond the enclosed left path from Hennock in nearly half a mile on the same lane and following the directions in No. 3; or if the rather more than two miles of lane to Chudleigh Station is preferred, turn right from Five Lanes on the Newton Abbot road, left almost immediately down a green lane and bear right on joining another lane, finishing as directed for No. 3.

To complete the present ramble, turn right at the cross roads mentioned at the beginning of the previous paragraph and take a forward bye-lane when the road forks right. Views over Bovey Tracey to Haytor, etc., soon open up and it will be interesting to trace how far one has walked over the surrounding country. At the bottom of the lane, turn right through the old town, avoiding all right turnings as the road bears left, but taking the right forward road, after crossing the river, to Bovey Station on the right.

There is not much object in continuing to Brimley Halt, but if it is decided to do so bear left with the main road, instead of going forward to Bovey Station, and fork right in about 500 yards, the Halt being a few more hundred yards down this road.

Hay Tor, one of Dartmoor's many attractions and well within reach of the railway line at Bovey Tracey. Like so much of the Moor this famous attraction was widely advertised in GWR publications.
*Author*

The South Hams, "Garden of Devon", with its lush rural landscape and easy access to the sea was in direct contrast to the rugged grandeur of Dartmoor. Like the Moor, it was progressively opened up to tourism by the railway. In December 1893 the $12^{1}/_{2}$ miles of the GWR branch line from Brent to Kingsbridge make the South Hams considerably more accessible. Passing, en-route, delightful South Devon locations such as Loddiswell, Gara Bridge and Avonwick, the line offered up the character and beauty of the district with its orchards, giant elms, oaks, hedgerows and cottages. Reaching southward for the sea, the line terminated at Kingsbridge, a comfortable market centre, 'capital of the South Hams', and, as S P Mais described it, a place where "the sea just stops at the foot of the town".

To the south was Salcombe and the open sea. It could be reached from Kingsbridge by water or by road, one of the particular attractions of the area being the many inviting creeks that brought the sea inland thereabouts. 'The Englishman's love of the sea is sufficient explanation of the growth of Salcombe' as one guide book put it, whilst others gloried in the atmosphere and setting. As a small town 'squeezed between the hillside and the water', Salcombe was likened to Mediterranean resorts'. *Seaside Watering Places*, 1904, was of this persuasion:

> Here the aloe and agave blossom, oranges, lemons and citrons flourish in the open air, and fuchsias grow to trees. The dianthus, blue gum tree, myrtle and camelia are common in almost every garden.

Rare butterflies and extensive varieties of fern embellished the exotic imagery. Fulsome comparisons on climate were made with Montpellier and, nearer home, with Falmouth and Penzance in the far West.

Timely action by the National Trust during the inter-war years safeguarded the coastline to Bolt Head ensuring that it did not fall victim to the inevitable 'developers' of that time. It was, of course, the varied attraction of the district, with it combination of classic rural Devon, inland, and spectacular cliffs, beaches and estuaries, at

the coast, that made Salcombe and the South Hams, generally, so desirable. Indeed, as *The Tourist's Guide to South Devon*, 1878, predicted: "If Salcombe were better known and more readily accessible, it would have no lack of visitors".

## COACHING EXCURSIONS THROUGH THE SOUTH HAMS.

### COACHES FROM KINGSBRIDGE STATION.

Combined Rail and Coach Tickets are issued every week-day as follows :—To Kingsbridge by Rail. Kingsbridge to Dartmouth by Coach *via* Torcross and Slapton. Return by Rail from Dartmouth or vice versa. The following are the fares:

| FROM | Inclusive fare for Rail and Coach Trip. | FROM | Inclusive fare for Rail and Coach Trip. |
|---|---|---|---|
| Devonport | | Saltash | |
| Plymouth (Millbay) | | Keyham | 6/- |
| North Road | 5/6 | | |
| Mutley | | Newton Abbot | |
| Plympton | | Lustleigh | |
| Ivybridge | | Bovey | |
| Brent | | Torre | |
| Avonwick | | Torquay | |
| Gara Bridge | | Paignton | |
| Loddiswell | 5/- | Churston | |
| Kingsbridge | | Brixham | 5/- |
| Totnes | | Kingswear | |
| Ashburton | | Dartmouth | |
| Buckfastleigh | | Starcross | |
| Moretonhampstead | 5/6 | Dawlish | |
| Exeter, St. Davids | | Teignmouth | |
| „ St. Thomas | | Chudleigh | |

### COACH FARES ONLY 3/6 IN EACH DIRECTION.

Tickets at the same fares as those shewn against Exeter, Torquay, and Plymouth can be previously obtained at the G.W. Offices at 107, Old Town Street, Plymouth; 97, Queen Street, Exeter; Vaughan Parade, Torquay; and 96, Fore Street, Devonport.

The Circular Trip Tickets are available for two days, so that Passengers can break the journey at Kingsbridge, Torcross, Slapton, or Dartmouth the first day, and return on the second day. Tickets taken on a Saturday may be used on the return journey on the following Monday. If any passenger should desire to make the double journey the same day on the Coach, and return to destination the same way he came, he may do so on paying to the Coach driver 2/6 extra.

In association with the Cheap Tickets issued to Kingsbridge (for particulars see excursion programme) the following Coach Trips are run on week-days from Kingsbridge to Torcross and Slapton Sands, and back :—The Coaches leave Kingsbridge Station at about 9.40 a.m. and 2.20 p.m., and return from Slapton Sands at about 5.20 p.m., Torcross 5.50 p.m., to Kingsbridge Station in time to catch the evening train.

Combined tickets embracing the Rail and Coach journeys are issued from the Plymouth Stations by certain morning trains. Third Class fare 4/6 inclusive.

**Proprietors of Coaches from Kingsbridge Station—**
THE DARTMOUTH COACHING CO. (Manager: Mr. Vickery, Torcross Hotel).

*For full particulars apply for programme of Rail, River and Coach Trips obtainable free of charge at the Stations, or post free from the Superintendent of the Line, Paddington, Station, W.*

### COACHES BETWEEN KINGSBRIDGE AND SALCOMBE.

Coaches are run daily between Kingsbridge and Salcombe in connection with the Company's trains. For full particular see information under heading of "Coaches" in G.W.R. Official Time Table.

Kingsbridge, seen here in May 1956, was the nearest the railway ventured to the South Devon resort of Salcombe, described by the GWR as "Britain's Most Southerly Resort." The terminus was host to many definitive features of the busy West Country branch line, as seen here in the station building, the goods yard, engine shed and carriage shed (a corrugated iron structure) along with other such familiar items as the half-harp gas lamps. All of this, once taken for granted, ordinary and functional in itself, now represents a lost, fond image of a branch line England where leisurely trains simmer quietly in the warmth of the summer sun, and all is well with the world.

*P. Gray*

For Information apply - Entertainments
Manager - GUILDHALL - PLYMOUTH

# PLYMOUTH

THE HOE
BATHING POOL

Moving westward, Plymouth, as a city, presented a very different prospect, underlining the rich diversity of landscape and experience offered in Devon. Rich in maritime history – Drake and the Armada, the Pilgrim Fathers, an emigration station, the Royal Dockyards and, from the mid-nineteenth century, an international packet station, and a prestigious trans-Atlantic steamer trade, Plymouth was a gateway to the rest of the world.

Great Western Railway publicity made much of Plymouth as an international seaport, offering its passengers the highest standards in both maritime and railway enterprise. The city also acted as a busy centre for coastal pleasure steamers, and for river excursions, locally. Giving details of the seasonal trips available in the early part of this century, an early volume of *Seaside Watering Places* maintained:

> Hardly a day passes without an excursion by steamer to one of the following places: Up the Yealm giving time to land at Newton Ferrers and occasionally as far as Salcombe and Kingsbridge, Dartmouth, Torquay and Fowey, Rame Head, Whitesand Bay, Eddystone Lighthouse, Looe; or a river excursion up the Tamar, under Brunel's railway bridge at Saltash to Cothele House, Calstock, Morwell Rocks and Wier Head; or by boat to St Germans on the River Lynher, passing the woods of Antony and Trematon and Ince Castle.

*The GWR Magazine* of July 1935 also related Plymouth's holiday attractions:

> A large new circular pool, a promenade and a colonnade are being built in the rocky face of the cliffs at the foot of the famous Hoe. The cliffs are now honey-combed with bathing and sun

bathing terraces, pools, shoots and diving boards and in the perfect setting of Plymouth Sound, the foreshore outrivals many of the much vaunted Mediterranean resorts".

Navy Week at Plymouth was also a great attraction. In the week, July 30 – August 6, 1938, for example, 9,935 people were brought to the port in 21 special trains.

A short but telling notification in the 1947 edition, the last of *Holiday Haunts* under the GWR, reminded potential visitors to Plymouth of the city's immediate post-war problems, having suffered extensive damage by the Luftwaffe in the early Spring of 1941.

---

# CITY OF PLYMOUTH

## *Notice to Intending Visitors*

The Lord Mayor, Aldermen, Councillors and Citizens present their compliments to Intending Visitors and regret that owing to enemy action the accommodation now available is strictly limited. It is confidently hoped, however, that in the not too distant future the City will again be able to offer ample accommodation and attractions for Visitors to this most beautiful part of the country.

Totnes: the well-known Butterwalk, reflecting the attraction of the town whose historic appeal was to make such a useful asset for GWR publicity purposes.

Both the Great Western and the Southern Railway provided main line services to Plymouth as would be expected of such an important city. In North Devon, however, the Southern Railway, inheriting the territory of the old London and South Western Company, was the major influence. This was also the case beyond Exeter, to the east of the River Exe.

Of the resorts on the north coast, Ilfracombe was the largest and best known. Like Cornwall, the north coast offered a very different atmosphere and experience from that of the south. The 1904 edition of *Seaside Watering Places* evidently approved of Ilfracombe as a place offering something for everyone. In its general atmosphere, facilities and image, the resort embodied the essential style of tourism definitive of the period right through from the early part of the century until the late fifties and early sixties. It was comfortable, confident, but not assertive; most of all it was characteristically English.

The season proper lasts from July to the end of September, May, June and July being the best months for visitors. The promenade pier is an extensive jetty running out from the harbour and affording landing stages at all tides. This is a very pleasant promenade, the constant arrival and departure of steamers, yachts etc. giving a moving interest to the scene, while Hillsborough on the other hand, and the town with its terraces and gardens afford a varied view. There are few pleasanter places for a morning or evening lounge than the pier and Lantern Hill. The Capstone Parade is, however, the principal resort of visitors on summer evenings, nor is this a matter of surprise; the hill juts out into the sea and starting from nearly sea level, broad paths are cut out of the rock, and rise by gradual ascents to a height of about 200 feet. On the lower promenade a band

Two views of Ilfracombe, North Devon's best known resort. The first view shows the harbour and Capstone Hill; the paddle steamer here reminding us that excursion traffic by sea was a particular feature of holidays at Ilfracombe. The second view shows the sea front area with the Victoria Pleasure Gardens, Pavilion and parade.

*The Homeland Association*

The 11.05 a.m. Ilfracombe-Wolverhampton headed by 4300 Class 2-6-0 No. 7337 runs through Milverton on 20 July 1963. Services began between Taunton and Barnstaple on 1 November 1873. Milverton gained a passing loop soon after this with further development in the mid thirties when the loop was extended (1936) and the station marked the end of a new section of double track running westward from Norton Fitzwarren, completed early in 1937.
*P. Gray*

East Anstey, looking westward, as 4300 Class 2-6-0 No. 7337 hurries the 8.35 a.m. Ilfracombe-Manchester through the station on 7 July 1962. This station marked a summit of sorts, the train having climbed the valley of the River Yeo on gradients varying between 1 in 58 and 1 in 70, it would then descend on a further lengthy section, again at 1 in 58, crossing into Somerset and heading for Dulverton en route. The passing loops here were also extended for the purposes of through summer traffic in 1937, and a camping coach was located here soon after.
*P. Gray*

performs morning and evening. The Victoria Promenade is a handsome glass and iron structure at the foot of the Capstone, on the south side, erected in 1887, and is a great acquisition when the winds are cold or there is a shower of rain. Concerts are also given here twice a day . . .

There are two bathing beaches at Ilfracombe . . . one at the Tunnels, where several acres are enclosed by a sea wall and with separate beaches for ladies and gentlemen, and the other at Rafferce Cove, near the harbour. At the back of the Ilfracombe Hotel there is a fine covered swimming bath 150ft. by 80ft. This is filled at every tide and is much appreciated. Separate hours are allotted for ladies.

Delightful walks and excursions can be taken in the neighbourhood, among them a short walk to Hillsborough, a bold hill 445 feet high, from which an extensive sea view can be had. On a clear day the coast of Wales can be plainly seen. The Torrs Walks, cut upon the sea face of conical hills lying to the west of the town afford grand views of the coast and sea, and the hills upon which they are cut are covered with fern and wild flowers in great variety. The coastline, being bold and rocky, is the habitat of innumerable sea birds; ferns also grow luxuriantly.

Described as 'the Torquay of North Devon', Ilfracombe's early visitors came mainly by sea. The railway from Exeter to Barnstaple, opened in 1854, was not extended to the resort until July 1874. The arrival of the railway obviously enhanced Ilfracombe's image and circumstances as a resort. Population figures from the mid nineteenth century to the years immediately following World War One are as follows:

1851 – 3,677
1861 – 3,851
1871 – 4,721
1881 – 6,255
1891 – 7,692
1901 – 8,557
1911 – 8,935
1921 – 11,772

The Great Western Railway's route from Taunton to Barnstaple opened in November 1873. Through trains from June 1887, off the Great Western bringing passengers from the Midlands and North, as well as those competing over rival routes from London, offered easier access, again, to Ilfracombe. Considerable work was carried out by the GWR in the 1930s to improve the Taunton-Barnstaple line reflecting the popularity of Ilfracombe, the line being kept busy until the early mid-1960s.

Ilfracombe itself did much to attract tourists. Municipal initiative in the inter-war years meant extensions to the promenade in 1928, and improvements to the Parade in 1932, with the opening of the Southern Slope Gardens – a rockery, waterfall, and shelters. Bowling and putting greens, and tennis courts, together with gardens were also provided by the local authority, the latter again purchasing practically the whole seaboard from Torrs Walk to Hele Beach, a distance of about two miles, The guide books from the inter-war years made much of this local authority initiative, an undoubted asset to North Devon's largest resort.

Steamer services to Lundy Island, to the South Wales resorts, and to the area's most famous locations, Clovelly and Lynton and Lynmouth, again did much to enhance Ilfracombe as an important centre for popular excursions. The railway also offered direct access to the remarkable Braunton Burrows and Saunton Sands, favourite locations for S P Mais when writing for the Southern Railway during the thirties.

Mortehoe on 27 July 1963 with 4300 Class 2-6-0 No. 6346 leaving for Ilfracombe on the 8.50 a.m. service from Taunton. The train will, thereafter, begin the descent of the formidable three-mile section, much of it at 1 in 36, to North Devon's principal holiday resort.
*P. Gray*

Eastward across the Devon-Somerset border and the heights of Exmoor, Minehead, Dunster and the Quantock countryside offered its particular charms. This was very much Great Western Railway territory and the Company made much of the decided atmosphere and character of rich landscape, peace and plenty. The spirit of the Quantocks was, in Great Western literature, guaranteed to please. Maxwell Fraser's evocative writing (*Somerset, GWR 1934*) was definitive of the period between the wars when the endless fascination with the English countryside and its rich association with the past enjoyed widespread acclaim and irresistable appeal:

In some curious way, the Quantocks impress even the casual visitor with their air of rich contentment. It is not merely that nature has been prodigal in her gifts to this lovely fertile range of hills, but that an air of happy serenity penetrates to every village, and climbs to the heights where long stretches of heather and bracken seem as fresh and untouched as in the days when the world was young. There is an atmosphere which suggests the fullness of contentment which we associate with the spacious days of Elizabeth, when England could lay just claim to the title of 'merry', and quaint customs and age-old traditions were maintained as a matter of course. Whilst so much of the rest of England is being modernised, life flows on among these lovely hills with a placidity born of prosperity and quiet content. Rich manor houses,

fine old farms, and charming cottages are to be seen, but no factories or even town to disturb the suggestion of ancient peace and plenty.

Here was the image of England that the Great Western nourished, careful also, of course, to acknowledge the ready availability of discreet but very modern amenities. What else, after all, was its purpose, but to provide the best possible service for the best possible people to the best possible places?

Minehead, the terminus of the line from Taunton through the Quantocks to the 'Severn Sea' coast, exemplified the image of hospitable charm together with sufficient concessions to the twentieth century to attract a broad base of popularity and consent. The resort proclaimed its seaside identity in its pier and promenade. It was much visited by steamers plying the Bristol Channel passages to neighbouring English and Welsh resorts. In 1936 the Great Western Railway's Chairman, Sir Robert Horne opened the resort's new swimming pool. This open-air structure, said to have cost £20,000, was described as "one of the finest in the country."

Quay Town and High Town were the particular delights of Minehead, at least to the writer of the GWR's *Somerset Ways* (1928).

It is indeed a pleasant place but there is much more in it than that, for it abounds with pictures, not in its main streets perhaps but in the by-ways where Old Somerset lingers. Of all these pictures, none remains more vivid than that of Quay Town, a cluster of ancient cottages grouped at the foot and on the lower slopes of North Hill, vividly white and cream against the dark green background of the Firs and sending each of them a spiral of clear blue peat smoke upward.

And there is quaintness and beauty in High Town, the oldest part of Minehead. Grouped around the magnificent church are cottages of true West Country type, with thatch, long chimneys and clean whitewashed fronts. Between the cottages leads a pathway set with shallow steps because it is so steep, upward to the Church – Minehead's proudest possession – a building impressive anywhere, but doubly so here, perched high on the hillside looking out over the sea, and landward over the sea flats and meadows to the rounded barrier of the Quantocks.

Minehead successfully combined its 'quaint' and 'mellow' manner with a definite element of modern tourist attractions. The council purchased 12 acres of pinewood on North Hill setting out attractive walks, with new gardens on the lower slopes above the harbour, and elsewhere in the town. This was noted with some satisfaction in the *GWR Magazine* for 1935, with a further report, in July 1936, recording the opening of the new open-air swimming pool. Butlin's Holiday Camp opened in 1962.

The writer of *Somerset Ways* gave pride of place in that part of the book to Dunster. Having conveyed the glory of nearby Cleeve Abbey and extolled the delights of coastline and the rural communities inland, the reader finds them but the prelude to the beauty of Dunster:

And here one must stay the pen a moment, for fear of too many words with but a little meaning for it is difficult to write in measured terms of this town – village, where all the most perfect beauty

Minehead promenade and North Hill, the latter often being a prominent feature in portraying the town. Promoted as a resort and as the 'Gateway to Exmoor', this turn of the century view was adapted in various ways by Great Western publicists.

Dunster, Yarn Market & High Street.

Dunster: a celebrated GWR location. This view from the 1920s looks along the main street with the ancient Yarn Market and the castle, through the trees beyond.

of the centuries is gathered up preserved and consecrated. For here is the Queen Village.

Two extracts from *Somerset Ways* in praise of Dunster must suffice here. As always with the GWR writers of the period, their imagery, style and chosen subject contributed to a glorious vision of England; a celebration of the senses:

The mile-long walk from the railway station to Dunster is down a shady field-fringed road, fragrant with meadowsweet. Then a few scattered cottages, quaint beyond words; a sharp turn, and one stands at the head of Dunster street, most perfect street man ever gazed on.

Wide in Dunster town, very wide, and the white, dark gabled cottages seem to have stood here since the world began so natural are they in their two uneven rows, uneven because no two adjacent houses are alike, in height or roof pitch, only in whitened front, dark tiled roof, lattice-paned windows and tiny gardens in the paving of the street. Straight in the broad street, high at the near end, where stand the Yarn Market, a circular open barn, perfect in form and texture; gently the street dips down, and then sweeps to the foot of Castle Hill. Each line, every cottage, leads the eye to Castle Hill, where, rising from the lovely woods which clothe it and form the background, the castle stands, strayed from a child's fairy dream, a white and stately miracle.

Minehead in the early years of nationalisation. A 2251 Class 0-6-0 waits with a stopping service for Taunton. The Minehead line was extensively improved during the thirties with extended sections of double track and passing loops at intermediate stations, together with the enlargement of the terminus itself. *N.R.M.*

Every cottage in the street might claim a chapter to itself, so varied, so perfect are they. Inside they more than fulfil the promise of their low-beamed entrance ways and quaint West Country chimneys. Low are the rooms with oaken beams polished by centuries of smoke, and by the reflection of domestic peace. Steps up and steps down, wide open hearths, twisting passages and stairways, and doors swinging on long hinges, old as history.

Harmonies of light and shadow, plenty and peace abounded in this homage to Old England where one would be "glad to sit for ever and dream what the world might be." Beyond the town itself was a landscape, equally magnificent:

The country around Dunster is a fit setting for the Queen Village, and is varied as the sky in May. Here are deep stream-laved valleys, dark with the shade of close-growing forest trees; shallow cup-like vales, with meandering, willow-fringed streams; and ploughed land where the wheat stands stiff and golden, and the silver blue oats stir and quiver with every lazy breath of the summer wind.

The Vale of Taunton and the town itself was another such location, again, quintessentially English. That this part of England was so well served by, and closely identified with, the GWR was a matter of pride and prestige for the Company, anxious always to be associated with rich and historic landscapes. This was conveyed to best effect by Maxwell Fraser in the chapter

on the Vale of Taunton Deane, from her book: *Somerset*. The Company chose well with this particular author, her style and content reflecting a definitive mood and atmosphere of the times. As one would expect, a strong sense of the character of the landscape was prominent, incorporating distinguished historical setting and associations. Taunton's role as a centre for tourism was also featured.

The countryside of the Vale of Taunton Deane is essentially serene and contented. It has the rich fertility which makes for an opulent pastoral beauty. Cows graze knee-deep in lush grass, tangled with delicate wild flowers. Hedges bloom with hawthorn, dog-roses and honeysuckle, or glow with berries. Orchards are fragrantly lovely with blossom-laden boughs or heavy with ripe fruit, and nightingales sing in the coppice. Mellow old farmhouses and sturdy cottages are trim and picturesque, reflecting the prosperity of their owners, and everywhere there is happy laughter and a rich contentment.

Cradled in the shelter of the Blackdowns, Brendons and Quantock Hills, and watered by the placid River Tone, the Vale hides in its heart the delightful old county town of Taunton. – Even in modern times it is essentially an agricultural town, and the chief outlet for the rich produce of the Vale. It suggests sturdy independence and simple yet ample comfort and is one of the friendliest and most lovable towns in the kingdom, and an incomparable touring centre.

One of Taunton's familiar 2251 Class 0-6-0s No. 2214 waits at no. 3 bay platform with a Taunton-Barnstaple branch train in July 1947. A Minehead train headed by 5100 Class 2-6-2T No. 4113 can also be seen in No. 4 Bay.

*Roger Venning*

An early post-war view of a Paddington-Minehead express gaining access to the branch at Norton Fitzwarren. Headed by GWR Prairie 5100 Class, 2-6-2T, No. 5172, of Taunton shed, this summer Saturday working of 6 September 1947 carries an 'M' identification disc to assist the signalmen along this crowded, hectic section of line at that time.

*Roger Venning*

Having completed oiling duties, the driver returns to 'County' No. 1011, *County of Chester* (not named at this time, being five months in service) to take his train away from Taunton's platform No. 7. This was a Penzance-North of England express, seen here on 2 June 1946.

*Roger Venning*

The Locomotive Exchanges of 1948. Ex LNER Pacific and record-breaker No. 22 *Mallard* is seen here leaving Taunton with the 8.30 a.m. Plymouth-Paddington. This train was regularly rostered for an 'exchange' locomotive, *Mallard*, here, being the subject of considerable attention.

*Tony Harvey Collection*

This celebration of image and things English was put to another practical, indeed, patriotic purpose in 1932. In that year with Britain's economy in deep depression, 'Holiday Haunts' included the following statement:

The 1932 edition of Holiday Haunts should have a very special appeal, since this year the national interest decisively indicates a British holiday for British holidaymakers. This well-known guide describes and illustrates the best of English holiday districts in a way such as will convince its readers that their patriotic duty will also be a pleasure.

Tourist traffic was a GWR success story particularly when contrasted with the ailing condition of the South Wales coal trade, for example. In an article outlining the growth and appeal of these tickets the GWR Magazine had the pleasant task of reporting success. Comparing 1930 with 1934 it seemed that this aspect of the tourist trade was in good shape.

In 1930 the number of Holiday Season Tickets issued by the Great Western Railway was 2,875. Last year the figure rose to 46,998, which was an increase of sixteen hundred per cent in the four years.

The reason for this striking success is that the Holiday Season Ticket represents the cheapest form of travel for holidaymakers who, for as little as fifteen shillings (first class) and ten shillings (third class), may travel at will for seven days and visit all the places worth seeing, over a wide area.

These tickets are free from restrictions; no trains are barred; break of journey is allowed at any point on route, and its period of availability may start on any day of the week . . .

Devon has three areas. One covers Torbay and Dartmoor and radiates from Newton Abbot to such places as Torquay, Kingswear, Paignton, Teignmouth, Dawlish, Chudleigh, Moreton-hampstead, Totnes and Ashburton. Another extends from St. Budeaux, west of Plymouth to Dawlish Warren, taking in the Kingsbridge and Ashburton branch and the Torbay district to Kingswear.

The third extends east from Newton Abbot to Taunton and Dulverton and includes Teignmouth, Dawlish, Exeter and Tiverton. . .

The extended Somerset and Devon area now covers the Quantock Hills, and the fringe of Exmoor and includes Taunton, Wellington, Minehead, Dulverton, Chard, Somerton, Weston Super Mare, Clevedon, Cheddar, Wookey and Wells.

Such facilities combined an easy mobility with an obvious economy, opening out all the GWR territory without restrictions. Accompanying publicity stressed the sense of freedom and adventure offered by these tickets with their provision for cyclists and for dog owners to include their animals in their visits.

**START YOUR RUN IN THE COUNTRY**

CHEAP RETURN FARES FOR YOU AND YOUR CYCLE

GWR

ENQUIRE AT THE STATION.

focussed on the historical, cultural traditions of Somerset, Devon and Cornwall. Leaving Paddington at 9.15a.m. the first destination was Bath, thence Minehead, Ilfracombe, Tintagel and Torquay, the latter offering the opportunity to visit historic Exeter and enjoy the celebrations for the eighth centenary of the cathedral. Cruise No. 3 also returned to Paddington from Torquay on the Saturday 'Torbay Express' at midday. A further option, Land Cruise No.5, was a virtual combination of Nos. 2 and 3. In the Company's own words it was "designed for those who wish to devote an unbroken fortnight to such a holiday (with) provision for two unorganised days, Saturday and Sunday, at Torquay with headquarters at the Grand Hotel." Torquay obviously played an important role in the Land Cruise concept. It was just over $3\frac{1}{2}$ hours from London, and along with its 'strategic' setting within the region overall, the resort reflected the image and experience of the 'English Riviera', a source of prestige and pride for all concerned. South Devon and Cornwall also featured prominently as 'Winter Resorts', the GWR being anxious to present its West Country resorts in the most favourable light. To this end, the Company emphasised the mild climate and medicinal properties readily available at such relatively close proximity to London and other large centres of population, and at no great inconvenience or cost.

Another means of holidaymaking actively promoted by the Great Western from 1934 was that of the camping coach. These were a great success in their first year and for 1935 there was additional accommodation, more camping coaches with improved facilities. Within the area covered by this book, there were, in 1935, coaches at Blue Anchor, near Minehead in West Somerset, and at Bampton, Dawlish Warren, Ide, Lustleigh and Avonwick in Devon. By 1938 the GWR offered extra locations – Stogumber in West Somerset and Ashton, East Anstey, Gara Bridge, Loddiswell, Princetown and Thorverton. The coaches came in four types, A-D. Type A was six-berth accommodation at a cost of £3 per week with a minimum of four rail tickets needed to qualify. Type B was again, six-berth at three pounds per week, four tickets being required. Type C was eight-berth at four pounds per week, six tickets required here. Type D, the only one in this classification being at Dawlish Warren, offered ten berths at five pounds, with eight tickets required to qualify.

Camping coaches reflected the thirties vogue for freedom, independence and activity together with the novelty element which was bound to appeal to those in search of something modern and, therefore, different in holiday terms. The camping coach provided a useful variation on the widespread camping craze of the period allowing the occupants to indulge their images of freedom and self expression without the necessary rigours of a robust full-scale regime under canvas. By 1959 *Holiday Haunts* listed Buckfastleigh, Dawlish Warren (eight coaches), Gara Bridge (two coaches), Loddiswell (two coaches) and Yealmpton (two coaches) as Western Region sites in Devon.

Tourism had considerable impact during the inter-war years showing that as an industry it had tremendous potential. By 1939 the Great Western was making definite efforts to encourage a longer season, appealing to tourists to take earlier holidays, in May and June, likewise, in September. Business was obviously good, as reflected in official figures from the Ministry of Labour

Another more expensive alternative for discovering the West of England was offered in the form of the GWR Land Cruise. Five cruises were available covering the various locations and landscapes of the Great Western Railway. Cruises numbers Two and Three concentrated on the West Country. "Paddington is the starting point for all the GWR land cruises" proclaimed the Company Magazine of 1931. Full details were given in an article of 1933. For Cruise No. 2, Torquay was the starting and finishing point within the area, passengers travelling there on the Monday via the prestigious 'Torbay Express.' From Torquay, passengers travelled by coach, the first night being spent at the resort thence travelling on at 9.30a.m. on the Tuesday to Newquay. The route was across Dartmoor to Tavistock, Launceston and Bodmin. One notable call en-route was made at Buckfast Abbey, a Benedictine Order established at Buckfastleigh and newly consecrated in 1932. The cruise then sampled the delights of the Cornish Riviera before returning to Plymouth for Friday. A short run on Saturday morning to Torquay offering the experience of Devon's magnificent South Hams landscape returned passengers to Torquay to join the Torbay Express, due back in Paddington at 3.35p.m.

Whilst Cruise No. 2 concentrated on the contrast and experience of landscape in its various moods and styles, the lush Devon pastoral experience and the magnificent dramatic qualities of the Cornish coastline, No. 3

5100 Class 2-6-2T No. 4145 leaves Dawlish Warren with the 9.20 a.m. Taunton-Goodrington Sands on 3 July 1957. Note the camping coach, one of seven at this extremely popular seaside location.
*R. C. Riley*

Gara Bridge typified the GWR rural station. Set amongst this rich and wonderfully wooded landscape of the South Hams, 4500 Class No. 4561 leaves the station with the 2.30 p.m. service for Brent on 8 June 1961. Note the two camping coaches in the station yard – an ideal setting for a country holiday.
*P. Gray*

and in statements from the Great Western management on the increasing difficulties in moving large numbers of people at the peak periods in late July and August. According to Ministry of Labour figures for 1939, 7,750,000 people out of a workforce of 18,500,000 qualified for paid holidays. This represented an increase of 1 million over 1938 and more than 2½ million over 1937. These figures were quoted by the GWR who went on to consider the logistics and practicalities of this situation in an article for the Company Magazine in 1939.

The question of transport for this ever increasing number of potential holiday-makers and their families inevitably arises and while the railway companies can carry them in comfort during the early summer or autumn it will be impossible to do so with the same degree of comfort if the convention of the August holiday is adhered to.

For years the Great Western Railway has advocated earlier holidays and was, in fact, the pioneer in this movement which has now assumed national importance.

World War Two put the problem to one side, whereafter, up until the early 1960s, tourism intensified, reaching a peak in the mid to late 1950s. In attempting, annually, to meet the demand, the railways were very much victims of their own success. Taking Torbay as an example, we can look at the numbers of people visiting Torquay on peak Summer Saturdays in 1957. According to the local press, reporting a statement from Torquay Station Master, Mr G O Collins, 80,838 passengers arrived at Torquay on the nine Saturdays beginning June 14. These peak figures also reflected the impact of a bus and coach strike that forced people onto trains but numbers for the corresponding period in 1958 showed that 75,951 people came to Torquay by train.

A survey of the number of trains in and out of neighbouring Paignton in 1959 reflects the intensity and diversity of summer Saturday services to and from all parts of Britain. The following tables, of course, do not include the numerous extra, relief trains to these services, making the achievement that much more impressive. Consider also, the record of Newton Abbot handling all this, and the extensive traffic to and from Plymouth and Cornwall, double-heading over the formidable South Devon banks.

Such details as these inevitably speak volumes for the attractions of Torbay and the West Country generally as Britain's premier holiday area. They also remind us of the phenomenal effort and workload taken up by railway employees struggling to meet these demands. If, indeed, Paignton and Torquay stations had been larger with a far more sophisticated infrastructure, the achievement would have been considerable, but given the confined circumstances for the railway at the two locations, the accomplishment was many times more worthy.

Plans had been prepared and some work begun at Paignton to modernise and extend facilities in the final years of peace leading to the outbreak of war. In the event, World War Two put a halt to all the Great Western's schemes for improvement, some of them being completed in the post-war period, others being lost to new and shifting circumstances of expediency, economy and change. Much had been done during the inter-war years to update the system with a view to the increasing demands of tourist traffic. Great Western investment during this period made it possible for this heavy holiday traffic to develop on the scale that has been indicated here, and it is to the GWR record of investment between the Wars that we now turn.

Climbing westward to Dainton Summit, 'Grange' No. 6855, *Saighton Grange,* and 'Modified Hall', No. 6988, *Swithland Hall,* pass Stoneycombe Quarry and signal box (the latter with reinforced flat roof) with the 'down' Cornish Riviera Express on Saturday 19 July 1958. The train ran non-stop from Newton Abbot to Truro, the 'King' on the run from Paddington had come off this train at Newton Abbot, to follow on a later working to Plymouth.

*R. C. Riley*

## PAIGNTON ARRIVALS

|  |  |
|---|---|
| 4.37 a.m. from Leicester London Road | dep 10.10 p.m. F.O. 1-29 August |
| 5.00 a.m. from Paddington | dep. 9.50 p.m. Sleeper to Newton Abbot |
| 5.10 a.m. from Wolverhampton | dep. 10.40 p.m. F.O. |
| 5.25 a.m. from Nottingham | dep. 10.00 p.m. F.O. Until 4/5 September |
| 5.30 a.m. from Paddington | dep. 11.35 p.m. Until 28/29 August |
| 5.47 a.m. from Sheffield | dep. 10.15 p.m. F.O. |
| 6.56 a.m. from Paddington | dep. 11.50 p.m. Sleeper to Newton Abbot |
| 7.03 a.m. from Bradford | dep. ? |
| 7.12 a.m. from Manchester | dep. 10.15 p.m. Until 21/22 August |
| 8.04 a.m. from Exeter | dep. 6.38 a.m. |
| 8.15 a.m. from Hull | dep. 10.10 p.m. Comm. 10/11 July F.O. |
| 8.35 a.m. from Manchester Victoria | dep. 11.15 p.m. Until 21/22 July |
| 8.50 a.m. from Newcastle | dep. 9.05 p.m. 26/27 June – 14/15 August |
| 9.20 a.m. from Exeter | dep. 8.00 a.m. |
| 10.10 a.m. from Glasgow - Plymouth connection | dep. 6.55 p.m. 26/27 June – 7/8 August |
| 10.35 a.m. from Cardiff | dep. 6.05 a.m. 25 July – 8 August |
| 11.08 a.m. from Exeter | dep. 9.30 a.m. |
| 11.45 a.m. from Paddington | dep. 7.00 a.m. |
| 11.56 a.m. from Paddington | dep. 7.40 a.m. 4 July – 29 August |
| 12.05 p.m. from Newport | dep. 8.10 a.m. Until 29 August |
| 12.38 p.m. from Cardiff | dep. 8.05 a.m. |
| 12.45 p.m. from Paddington | dep. 8.10 a.m. Until 5 September |
| 1.03 p.m. from Birmingham Moor Street | dep. 7.30 a.m. 18 July – 22 August |
| 1.23 p.m. from Walsall | dep. 6.35 a.m. |
| 1.30 p.m. from Wolverhampton | dep. 6.55 a.m. |
| 1.40 p.m. from Paddington | dep. 8.50 a.m. |
| 2.00 p.m. from Paddington | dep. 7.30 a.m. |
| 2.05 p.m. from Paddington | dep. 9.40 a.m. |
| 2.17 p.m. from Leicester | dep. 6.40 a.m. Until 29 August |
| 2.28 p.m. from Paddington | dep. 10.15 a.m. |
| 2.50 p.m. from Paddington | dep. 10.40 a.m. 4 July – 29 August |
| 3.22 a.m. from Swansea | dep. 9.05 a.m. |
| 3.35 p.m. from Wolverhampton | dep. 9.25 a.m. via Banbury 27 June – 5 September |
| 4.08 p.m. from Paddington | dep. 12.00 'Torbay Express' |
| 4.32 p.m. from Sheffield | dep. 8.00 a.m. |
| 4.50 p.m. from Wolverhampton | dep. 10.35 a.m. |
| 5.18 p.m. from Manchester | dep. 8.00 a.m. |
| 5.28 p.m. from Liverpool | dep. 8.35 a.m. |
| 5.46 p.m. from Manchester LR | dep. 9.00 a.m. |
| 5.57 p.m. from Paddington | dep. 1.25 a.m. |
| 6.15 p.m. from Newcastle | dep. 7.30 a.m. |
| 6.30 p.m. from Bradford | dep. 9.05 a.m. 'The Devonian' |
| 6.48 p.m. from Liverpool | dep. 9.05 a.m. |
| 7.44 p.m. from Paddington | dep. 3.15 p.m. |
| 8.05 p.m. from Bradford | dep. ? |
| 8.35 p.m. from Exeter | dep. 7.14 p.m. |
| 9.07 p.m. from Manchester LR | dep. 11.45 a.m. |
| 9.53 p.m. from Paddington | dep. 5.30 p.m. The Mayflower |
| 10.35 p.m. from Paddington | dep. 4.15 p.m. via Bristol |
| 12.08 a.m. from Newton Abbot – connection with Manchester - Plymouth service. | |

## PAIGNTON DEPARTURES

|  |  |  |
|---|---|---|
| Wolverhampton | dep. 11.50 p.m. | arr. 6.10 a.m. Friday/Saturday 7/8 August only |
| Taunton | dep. 5.40 a.m. | arr. 8.31 a.m. |
| Manchester Vic | dep. 6.35 a.m. | arr. 3.06 p.m. 25 July – 15 August |
| Bradford | dep. 6.50 a.m. | arr. 4.44 p.m. |
| Paddington | dep. 7.20 a.m. | arr. 12.15 p.m. |
| Exeter | dep. 7.45 a.m. | arr. 8.55 a.m. 20 June only |
| Newcastle | dep. 7.45 a.m. | arr. 7.13 p.m. From 27 June |
| Manchester Victoria | dep. 8.00 a.m. | arr. 4.27 p.m. Until 5 September |
| Paddington | dep. 8.18 a.m. | arr. 12.50 p.m. |
| Nottingham Mid | dep. 8.40 a.m. | arr. 4.35 p.m. |
| Sheffield Mid | dep. 8.50 a.m. | arr. 4.33 p.m. (To Leeds City arr. 6.00 p.m. 4 July to 5 Sept) |
| Manchester LR | dep. 9.05 a.m. | arr. 5.23 p.m. |
| Bradford | dep. 9.16 a.m. | arr. 7.02 p.m. The Devonian |
| Swansea | dep. 9.30 a.m. | arr. 3.15 p.m. 27 June – 5 September |
| Birmingham Moor St | dep. 9.40 a.m. | arr. 3.51 p.m. via Banbury 27 June – 5 September |
| Paddington | dep. 10.00 a.m. | arr. 2.20 p.m. |
| Cardiff | dep. 10.10 a.m. | arr. 2.55 p.m. |
| Wolverhampton | dep. 10.30 a.m. | arr. 5.12 p.m. |
| Liverpool | dep. 10.44 a.m. | arr. 7.48 p.m. |
| Nottingham Mid | dep. 10.55 a.m. | arr. 8.17 p.m. |
| Paddington | dep. 11.45 a.m. | arr. 4.10 p.m. Torbay Express |
| Cardiff | dep. 12.05 p.m. | arr. 4.31 p.m. 27 June – 29 August |
| Manchester | dep. 12.30 p.m. | arr. 10.07 p.m. |
| Wolverhampton | dep. 12.45 p.m. | arr. 7.22 p.m. |
| Paddington | dep. 1.30 p.m. | arr. 6.05 p.m. 4 July – 29 August |
| Paddington | dep. 1.45 p.m. | arr. 6.15 p.m. 20/27 June, 5/12 September |
| Wolverhampton | dep. 1.55 p.m. | arr. 7.50 p.m. |
| Paddington | dep. 2.00 p.m. | arr. 7.15 p.m. |
| Sheffield Midland | dep. 2.25 p.m. | arr. 9.49 p.m. |
| Paddington | dep. 3.05 p.m. | arr. 9.41 p.m. |
| Birmingham Moor St | dep. 2.50 p.m. | arr. 8.38 p.m. Until 29 August |
| Wolverhampton | dep. 3.05 p.m. | arr. 9.41 p.m. |
| Cardiff | dep. 3.50 p.m. | arr. 8.35 p.m. |
| Paddington | dep. 4.15 p.m. | arr. 8.50 p.m. |
| Taunton | dep. 4.40 p.m. | arr. 7.27 p.m. |
| Paddington | dep. 5.00 p.m. | arr. 9.20 p.m. |
| Nottingham | dep. 5.15 p.m. | arr. 12.56 a.m. 25 July – 29 August |
| Taunton | dep. 5.57 p.m. | arr. 9.16 p.m. |
| Exeter | dep. 6.55 p.m. | arr. 8.15 p.m. |
| Exeter | dep. 7.44 p.m. | arr. 9.00 p.m. |
| Sheffield | dep. 8.15 p.m. | arr. 4.45 a.m. 25/26 July – 8/9 August |
| Manchester | dep. 8.22 p.m. | arr. 6.39 a.m. Sleeper from Plymouth |
| Exeter | dep. 9.04 p.m. | arr. 10.20 p.m. |
| Exeter | dep. 10.02 p.m. | arr. 11.12 p.m. |
| Manchester/Liverpool | dep. 10.20 p.m. | arr. Manchester LR 7.08 a.m. Liverpool 6.58 a.m. 25/26 July – 15/16 August |

'Hall' No. 5920, *Wycliffe Hall,* lifts the 8.00 a.m. Paignton-Manchester up the 1 in 55 gradient between Torquay and Torre on 6 August 1960. With the briefest of respite at Torre, the gradient then eases back to 1 in 73 for almost another mile. For heavily loaded trains, starting out at the foot of the bank at Torquay, this ascent presented no easy options. Halls and Granges were allowed 320 tons unassisted; Castles, 345 tons, and Kings, 390 tons. With assistance to Torre advanced starter, permissible loadings were 420 tons, 455 tons and 500 tons, respectively.                                    *A. Fairclough Collection*

Newton Abbot, erstwhile railway centre of South Devon at its busiest. 'Castle' No. 7005, *Sir Edward Elgar* backs on to the 8.35 a.m. Birmingham-Paignton relief service on 19 July 1958.                                    *R. C. Riley*

## Chapter Three
# Prosperity and Progress
# – the Inter-War Years

Investment in West Country tourist traffic was a definitive feature of GWR policy in the inter-war years. A great deal was planned during this time to develop the trade, tourism being a valuable source of income in otherwise difficult times.

The first major project of the period was the rebuilding of Newton Abbot station undertaken between 1924 and 1927. This had been considered necessary in the years leading to 1914, but had to be delayed, making it an even greater priority by the twenties. Newton Abbot was the junction for the Torbay line and for the Moretonhampstead branch (with access to the Teign Valley line to Exeter). The station dated back through modifications in the 1860s to its original South Devon Railway lineage of 1846. It had only three running lines serving three platforms with which to handle the rapidly escalating passenger traffic.

Under redevelopment, the overall roof was demolished whilst the three platforms were replaced by two expansive island structures, each 1,375 feet in length with scissors cross-overs to enable maximum use at busy periods. Six lines were now available through the station; an 'up' through line, 'up' main platform, 'up' relief, 'down' relief and 'down' through line. At the east end of the station, on the up side, (the site of the former goods shed) a new separate bay platform of 320 feet was provided for the Moretonhampstead branch traffic. Substantial improvements for goods traffic had been completed in 1911 on a new site especially prepared alongside the Moretonhampstead branch and the River Teign, at a right angle to the station and main line.

Entry to the station was via the imposing three-storey structure of Portland stone and red Somerset brick. The company magazine gave the following description:

At street level there are booking and parcels offices, a spacious booking hall and cloakroom. Commodious refreshment rooms are available on each platform, also centrally placed waiting rooms and attractive bookstalls. The station is lighted by electricity, and all the buildings are centrally heated. On the first floor is a dining and tea room, 66 feet by 19 feet. This room will be available for social functions and has a separate entrance with staircase, which gives access to and from the street.

Reference to the premises being available for separate functions relates to the definite sense of partnership between the railway and the town. Much was made of this, the town preparing a portion of land for the approach road and station frontage, calculated to show the new building in the best possible light. The gift of clocks for the station, donated by the community in gratitude for the work carried out by the GWR, is a further instance of this relationship.

As the largest employer in this otherwise South Devon market town, the GWR had a considerable profile. The locomotive works, the recently enlarged freight depot and the new Hackney Yard of 1911 were vital sources of employment, the GWR having a wage-bill of £200,000 annually, employing over 900 people.

Railway development since the mid-nineteenth century assured that Newton Abbot would flourish as a market centre for the surrounding area; the railway geography guaranteed this.

In the same way, both the company and the town utilised this situation in terms of tourism. Portrayed as the "Gateway to Dartmoor" in railway terms, Newton Abbot proclaimed its unique position as a centre for various types of holidays; by the sea at Teignmouth or Torbay, or, inland amongst the historic South Devon towns, and, indeed, on Dartmoor itself. Whatever was desired, the town was ideally placed to meet it. The President of the Chamber of Commerce acknowledged the part played by the GWR in promoting the town, the occasion being the formal opening of the new station on Monday, 11 April 1927. In toasting the success of the company and the town he pointed out that in recent years the GWR had done as much as the town itself in advertising and had now put forward "a further generous offer towards a Press advertising campaign for Newton Abbot as a holiday centre for Devon."

Newton Abbot station itself, and the intense activity and excitement of a major railway centre, was proposed as a holiday location by one contributor to the *GWR Magazine* in 1931. Beatrice Chase, a well-known author of the period, wrote:

I cannot imagine a more wonderful holiday than to settle in at Newton Abbot station for a day. It meets with every requirement that a railway maniac like myself can desire.

All the most famous trains pass through or stop there. You can walk miles up and down the nine platforms. There are bookstalls laden with current fiction. Refreshment rooms welcome you. For the most serious business of lunch and tea there is the luxurious restaurant on the first floor . . . Weather does not affect the day's entertainment. If fine, you can haunt the open platforms. If wet, the covered ones, and there is warmth in all the waiting and refreshment rooms.

This is a familiar scenario to the countless thousands of railway enthusiasts who have, and continue to spend their time rail-side, but the extract also conveys the sense in which the station was a definitive part of the community, vibrant and dynamic.

Further east, reaching across the Devon-Somerset border, the Great Western introduced vital modernisation over the entire line between Cogload Junction, east of Taunton, (the site where the Paddington and Bristol lines converged, coming westward), and Norton Fitzwarren five miles west of Taunton. Other important, related works included the rebuilding of intermediate stations between Taunton and Exeter, in fact, reaching down the Exe estuary to Exminster. The bulk of the work was completed in 1931 and 1932, the stations involved being Norton Fitzwarren, Wellington, Sampford Peverell (now the site of Tiverton Parkway), the extensive redevelopment at Tiverton Junction, Cullompton, Stoke Cannon and, beyond Exeter, Exminster.   All these stations were given

The 12.15 p.m. Kingswear-Wolverhampton passes Newton Abbot East Box on its way to Exeter where it will join with the 10.30 a.m. Penzance-Wolverhampton – *The Cornishman*. This part of the service is headed by 'Castle' No. 5003 *Lulworth Castle*. 18 July 1956.                                                              *R. C. Riley*

Heathfield, on the Moretonhampstead branch and junction for the Teign Valley line to Exeter. This view, looking north, shows 0-4-2T 1400 Class No. 1472 with a Moretonhampstead-Newton Abbot train in 1958. The layout here dates from 1927 when the crossing loop and 'up' platform were provided; the main platform also serving the Teign Valley was extended and developed at this time. Further extension of the loop and improved access to and from the Teign Valley line took place during 1943. The latter work can be seen with the junction leading away to the right, north-eastward, immediately beyond the signal box. The Teign Valley line did not open throughout until 1 July 1903, but the first section, Heathfield to Ashton opened as a standard gauge service on 9 October 1882. Standard gauge services on this line stood alongside broad gauge trains to Moretonhampstead at Heathfield.          *P. Q. Treloar*

Cogload, the eastern limit for this survey. 'Bulldog' 4-4-0, No. 3443 *Chaffinch* pilots 'Star' 4-6-0 No. 4042, *Prince Albert* on the 'up' 8.30 a.m. Plymouth-Paddington on 11 September 1947. The train is passing beneath Cogload Flyover, a vital engineering initiative of the early thirties, built to carry the 'down' line from Bristol over the West of England main line, to and from Paddington. *Pursey Short*

Fairwater Bridge, west of Taunton station, with 'Castle' No. 5024, *Carew Castle* passing beneath with a summer Saturday Manchester-Penzance working on 13 September, 1947. The bridge was one of many structures to be rebuilt under the quadrupling programme of the early thirties. *Roger Venning*

through roads with platform loops to help ease the occupation of this section of main line, particularly for summer traffic.

Taunton was the focal point of Great Western development between Cogland and Norton Fitzwarren in the early thirties. Like Newton Abbot, it was a vital main line location with considerable local feeder lines; like Newton Abbot, Taunton was an important market centre for the area and, much more so, was the county town – the administrative and commercial capital. Together with its considerable main line traffic, Taunton was the junction for the branches to Barnstaple and Minehead to the west, and to Yeovil and Chard in the east.

Two years of extensive works carried out under the Development (Loans Guarantees and Grants) Act of 1929, commencing in September 1930 and completed in early February 1932, transformed the railway landscape locally. Working east-west, the project comprised the construction of a flyover at Cogload Junction carrying the 'down' Bristol line over the West of England main line from Paddington with quadruple track thereafter, through Taunton to Norton Fitzwarren segregating the Bristol and Paddington services. The 'up' and 'down' Bristol lines were obviously separated by the West of England line. Extensive work was required to make the embankments, estimated at 140,000 cubic yards, the numerous culverts, the sixteen bridges either newly built or reconstructed, and, of course, the signalling arrangements requiring several new signal boxes and the relocation of certain existing structures, that at Cogload Junction being an obvious example. The fly-over consisted of a steel bridge built on a skew, the main girders being 185 feet in length, south side, and 161 feet north side. A substantial retaining wall guarded the West of England main line and the embankment bringing west bound trains off the fly-over. The rising gradient on the Bristol side was much gentler than that falling towards Taunton.

Rebuilding work at Taunton station swept away the old site. A "substantial well proportioned, almost elegant station" with an overall roof had replaced the original single sided structure in August 1868. This, in turn, was much enhanced by further work in 1895. From this time, Taunton comprised 'up' and 'down' main platform with a centre line evidently not used for direct through services. The overall roof covered the central business area of the station, the platforms, extending some way beyond this in both directions, were protected by canopies. Bay platforms were also provided at each end of the station and on both sides of the line (1895). Goods avoiding lines and a new locomotive shed were also constructed at this time.

The two-year reconstruction, from 1930 to 1932, saw the removal of the overall roof and the provision of four main line platforms. An island platform served the up and down main, whilst the outer platforms were designated 'up' and 'down' relief lines. The platforms were linked by means of a new subway, 140 feet long and 15 feet wide. On the 'up' side, a new widened approach road led to the new booking hall and access up to the platform where, again, new refreshment, dining and waiting rooms were provided. Similar facilities were offered on the down platform where the original accommodation had been modernised and enlarged. Refreshment and waiting rooms were also provided on the island platform. Extensive provision for goods traffic was also part of the development at Taunton, including a new goods warehouse and yard, the latter to the west of the station, 'down' side.

The summer service of 1932, shown in the following tables, and the first to benefit from the investment programme in and around Taunton, records the intense pattern of long distance and local traffic. When considered in the overall context of the total traffic – through express workings, parcels, empty stock, perishables and, of course, considerable freight, the volume of traffic was impressive, and in later years, particularly the post-war period, peaking in the late 1950s, the investment was tested to its limits.

As a railway centre and a focal point for tourism, Taunton played an important part in GWR interests in the West of England. For the Great Western it was the undoubted gateway to the West.

**TAUNTON ARRIVALS AND DEPARTURES, EASTBOUND**

| | | |
|---|---|---|
| 12.10 a.m. | dep | – Penzance-Manchester L.R. Holiday Ticket Train, Fri only |
| 1.35 a.m. | arr | – Barnstaple – Fri/Sats only |
| 1.55 a.m. | dep | – Paignton-Manchester L.R. Holiday Ticket Train. Sat night only |
| 2.05 a.m. | dep | – Penzance-Paddington Holiday Ticket Train. Fri only |
| 2.39 a.m. | dep | – Penzance-Paddington – Sleeper Service |
| 5.50 a.m. | dep | – Chard |
| 6.50 a.m. | dep | – Bristol (Birmingham Mon, Fri, Sats) |
| 7.10 a.m. | dep | – Yeovil Pen Mill |
| 7.46 a.m. | arr | – Wellington |
| 8.00 a.m. | dep | – Bristol |
| 8.00 a.m. | dep | – Chard |
| 8.27 a.m. | dep | – Castle Cary |
| 8.34 a.m. | arr | – Barnstaple |
| 8.38 a.m. | arr | – Minehead |
| 8.45 a.m. | arr | – Exeter |
| 9.00 a.m. | dep | – Weston Super Mare |
| 9.15 a.m. | dep | – Paignton-Paddington Mon only |
| 9.15 a.m. | dep | – Paignton-Derby/Sheffield Holiday Ticket Train Sats only |
| 9.40 a.m. | dep | – Kingswear-Birkenhead, Liverpool, Manchester Friday and Saturdays |
| 9.40 a.m. | dep | – Paignton-Bristol, Monday to Thursday |
| 10.00 a.m. | dep | – Yeovil |
| 10.03 a.m. | arr | – Minehead |
| 10.10 a.m. | dep | – Taunton-Paddington |
| 10.16 a.m. | arr | – Exeter |
| 10.27 a.m. | arr | – Barnstaple |
| 10.30 a.m. | arr | – Minehead |
| 10.45 a.m. | dep | – Plymouth/Kingswear-Paddington |
| 10.50 a.m. | dep | – Chard |
| 10.55 a.m. | dep | – Bridgwater |
| 11.00 a.m. | dep | – Yeovil |
| 11.10 a.m. | dep | – Plymouth-Birkenhead, Liverpool, Manchester (Glasgow Sat exc) |
| 11.30 a.m. | dep | – Kingswear-Leeds, Bradford |
| 11.40 a.m. | dep | – Bristol |
| 11.43 a.m. | dep | – Castle Cary |
| 11.51 a.m. | arr | – Barnstaple Fri/Sats only |
| 12.04 p.m. | arr | – Exeter |
| 12.35 p.m. | dep | – Ilfracombe, Minehead-Paddington |
| 12.40 p.m. | dep | – Exeter-Liverpool Fri/Sats only |
| 1.00 p.m. | dep | – Penzance/Kingswear-Birmingham Sats exc Through coaches Birkenhead, Liverpool, Manchester |
| 1.08 p.m. | dep | – Chard |
| 1.20 p.m. | dep | – Yeovil Pen Mill |
| 1.35 p.m. | dep | – Penzance-Paddington, Saturdays excepted |
| 1.40 p.m. | dep | – Bristol Sat only |
| 1.56 p.m. | arr | – Exeter |
| 2.35 p.m. | dep | – Weston Super Mare, Sats only |
| 2.40 p.m. | dep | – Ilfracombe/Minehead-Paddington (Ilfracombe/Minehead Express) |

| 2.45 p.m. | dep | – Castle Cary |
| 3.04 p.m. | dep | – Paignton-Wolverhampton (Through carriage to Manchester L.R. Sats only) |
| 3.13 p.m. | dep | – Penzance, Newquay, Paignton-Liverpool (Through carriages Birkenhead), Manchester |
| 3.18 p.m. | dep | – Penzance-Bristol Sats only |
| 3.40 p.m. | dep | – Penzance, Newquay, Paignton-Wolverhampton Sats excluded |
| 3.45 p.m. | arr | – Minehead |
| 3.55 p.m. | dep | – Bristol Sats only |
| 4.02 p.m. | dep | – Penzance-Aberdeen Through coaches via Westbury, Banbury, York. Through coaches Westbury-Glasgow |
| 4.15 p.m. | dep | – Penzance, Plymouth, Paignton-Paddington |
| 4.20 p.m. | dep | – Yeovil |
| 4.25 p.m. | dep | – Chard |
| 4.30 p.m. | dep | – Penzance-Paddington |
| 4.40 p.m. | dep | – Castle Cary |
| 4.59 p.m. | arr | – Barnstaple |
| 5.09 p.m. | arr | – Exeter |
| 5.27 p.m. | dep | – Weston Super Mare |
| 5.30 p.m. | arr | – Minehead |
| 5.55 p.m. | dep | – Yeovil |
| 5.57 p.m. | arr | – Barnstaple |
| 6.10 p.m. | dep | – Penzance-Liverpool, Manchester, Glasgow |
| 6.23 p.m. | dep | – Penzance, Paignton, Ilfracombe-Paddington |
| 6.46 p.m. | dep | – Chard |
| 6.35 p.m. | dep | – Taunton-Birmingham Through coach from Ilfracombe |
| 6.40 p.m. | arr | – Barnstaple Sats only |
| 6.50 p.m. | dep | – Penzance-Paddington Holiday Ticket Train Sats only |
| 6.52 p.m. | dep | – Castle Cary |
| 7.10 p.m. | dep | – Bristol |
| 7.21 p.m. | arr | – Exeter |
| 7.47 p.m. | arr | – Minehead |
| 7.50 p.m. | dep | – Bridgwater |
| 7.52 p.m. | arr | – Barnstaple Sats exc |
| 8.06 p.m. | arr | – Plymouth N.R. |
| 8.15 p.m. | arr | – Barnstaple |
| 8.30 p.m. | dep | – Plymouth-Paddington Sats only |
| 8.40 p.m. | dep | – Penzance-Bristol. |
| 8.50 p.m. | dep | – Frome |
| 8.55 p.m. | dep | – Chard |
| 8.57 p.m. | arr | – Minehead |
| 9.00 p.m. | dep | – Yeovil Pen Mill |
| 9.42 p.m. | arr | – Kingswear |
| 10.22 p.m. | arr | – Minehead |
| 10.30 p.m. | dep | – Penzance-Manchester/Liverpool |
| 10.45 p.m. | arr | – Exeter Thurs, Sats exc |
| 11.00 p.m. | dep | – Keinton Mandeville |
| 11.10 p.m. | dep | – Chard Sats only |
| 11.12 p.m. | arr | – Minehead Fri/Sats only |
| 11.25 p.m. | arr | – Barnstaple Fridays only |
| 11.40 p.m. | dep | – Ilfracombe-Manchester Holiday Ticket Train Fridays only |

## TAUNTON ARRIVALS AND DEPARTURES, WESTBOUND

| 2.00 a.m. | arr | – Paddington-Penzance Sleeper – also through coaches from Aberdeen to Penzance |
| 3.00 a.m. | arr | – Manchester-Paignton Holiday Ticket Trains Fri only |
| 3.20 a.m. | arr | – Paddington-Ilfracombe/Kingswear Holiday Ticket Train Friday night only |
| 4.00 a.m. | arr | – Manchester Vic-Torquay, Penzance Holiday Ticket Train Fri only |
| 4.08 a.m. | arr | – Paddington-Penzance Saturday nights excepted |
| 4.25 a.m. | arr | – Paddington-Penzance Sleeper to Plymouth – Sat night excepted |
| 5.55 a.m. | arr | – East Lancs-Torquay Holiday Ticket Train Fri only Not after 26/27 August |
| 6.55 a.m. | dep | – Wellington |
| 7.05 a.m. | dep | – Exeter |
| 7.10 a.m. | dep | – Minehead |
| 7.33 a.m. | arr | – Liverpool, Manchester-Penzance |
| 7.50 a.m. | dep | – Barnstaple |
| 8.10 a.m. | dep | – Minehead |
| 8.41 a.m. | arr | – Bristol |
| 8.51 a.m. | arr | – Yeovil Pen Mill |
| 9.00 a.m. | dep | – Exeter |
| 9.05 a.m. | arr | – Manchester-Taunton Holiday Ticket Train Fri only Not after 26/27 August |

| 9.17 a.m. | arr | – Castle Cary |
| 9.18 a.m. | arr | – Chard |
| 9.25 a.m. | arr | – Bristol |
| 9.52 a.m. | arr | – Paddington-Penzance |
| 10.28 a.m. | dep | – Barnstaple |
| 10.35 a.m. | dep | – Exeter |
| 10.50 a.m. | dep | – Minehead |
| 10.52 a.m. | arr | – Swindon |
| 11.00 a.m. | arr | – Yeovil Pen Mill |
| 11.07 a.m. | arr | – Wolverhampton-Paignton |
| 11.30 a.m. | arr | – Paddington-Plymouth |
| 11.41 a.m. | arr | – Castle Cary |
| 11.52 a.m. | arr | – Paddington-Minehead, Ilfracombe, Kingswear |
| 12.00 noon | dep | – Exeter |
| 12.05 p.m. | dep | – Minehead |
| 12.07 p.m. | arr | – Weston Super Mare |
| 12.26 p.m. | arr | – Chard |
| 12.43 p.m. | arr | – Yeovil Pen Mill |
| 1.15 p.m. | dep | – Barnstaple |
| 1.36 p.m. | arr | – Swansea-Paignton Sats excepted Through carriage Plymouth on Fridays |
| 1.46 p.m. | arr | – Swansea-Paignton and Plymouth Saturdays only |
| 2.00 p.m. | arr | – Paddington-Penzance Saturdays excepted |
| 2.09 p.m. | arr | – Paddington-Penzance Saturdays only |
| 2.16 p.m. | arr | – Castle Cary |
| 2.36 p.m. | arr | – Wolverhampton-Torquay, Newquay, Penzance Saturdays excepted |
| 2.36 p.m. | arr | – Wolverhampton-Torquay, Paignton, Plymouth Saturdays only |
| 2.45 p.m. | arr | – Paddington-Ilfracombe Saturdays only |
| 2.47 p.m. | arr | – Chard |
| 3.00 p.m. | dep | – Exeter |
| 3.01 p.m. | arr | – Paddington-Minehead, Ilfracombe, Plymouth Saturdays only |
| 3.07 p.m. | arr | – Weston Super Mare Saturday excepted |
| 3.20 p.m. | arr | – Wolverhampton-Ilfracombe Saturdays only |
| 3.45 p.m. | arr | – Liverpool/Manchester- Paignton, Plymouth, Newquay, Truro |
| 3.55 p.m. | arr | – Yeovil |
| 4.05 p.m. | arr | – Manchester L.R.-Paignton Saturdays only |
| 4.14 p.m. | arr | – Paddington-Ilfracombe, Torquay, Newquay, Penzance |
| 4.33 p.m. | arr | – Nottingham/Derby-Paignton Saturdays only |
| 4.33 p.m. | arr | – Nottingham/Derby-Paignton, Plymouth Saturdays excepted |
| 4.45 p.m. | dep | – Minehead |
| 4.55 p.m. | dep | – Wellington |
| 4.56 p.m. | arr | – Bradford/Leeds-Paignton Through express Fri/Sat |
| 5.05 p.m. | arr | – Bradford/Leeds-Kingswear Through coaches Fri/Sats excepted |
| 5.20 p.m. | dep | – Minehead |
| 5.25 p.m. | arr | – Castle Cary |
| 5.34 p.m. | arr | – Weston Super Mare |
| 5.45 p.m. | dep | – Barnstaple |
| 5.56 p.m. | arr | – Chard |
| 6.00 p.m. | arr | – Paddington-Minehead, Ilfracombe, Torquay, Plymouth, Truro |
| 6.15 p.m. | dep | – Exeter |
| 6.30 p.m. | dep | – Minehead |
| 7.00 p.m. | arr | – Yeovil |
| 7.15 p.m. | arr | – Liverpool L.S.-Taunton |
| 7.51 p.m. | arr | – Paddington-Torquay, Plymouth |
| 8.03 p.m. | arr | – Castle Cary |
| 8.12 p.m. | arr | – Chard |
| 8.15 p.m. | dep | – Barnstaple |
| 8.20 p.m. | dep | – Kingswear |
| 8.30 p.m. | dep | – Minehead |
| 8.38 p.m. | arr | – Bristol |
| 8.58 p.m. | arr | – Yeovil Pen Mill |
| 10.05 p.m. | arr | – Paddington-Plymouth |
| 10.12 p.m. | arr | – Chard |
| 10.15 p.m. | arr | – Castle Cary |
| 10.41 p.m. | arr | – Birmingham |
| 10.50 p.m. | arr | – Chard |
| 11.00 p.m. | dep | – Minehead Saturdays only |
| 11.10 p.m. | dep | – Wiveliscombe Saturday only |
| 11.15 p.m. | dep | – Wellington (Tiverton Junction Saturdays only) |
| 12.34 a.m. | arr | – Chard Saturdays only |
| 12.55 a.m. | arr | – Bristol Saturdays only |

## Table 82 TAUNTON, WATCHET and MINEHEAD

| Miles | | MONDAYS TO FRIDAYS | | | | | | | | | | | | | SATURDAYS | | | | | | |
|---|---|---|---|---|---|---|---|---|---|---|---|---|---|---|---|---|---|---|---|---|---|
| | | am | am | | am | am | am | | pm | pm | pm | | pm | | am | am | am | am | am | am | am T |
| | 61 London (Pad.) 62 .. dep | .. | .. | .. | 5 30 | 9 30 | 11 30 | .. | .. | 1 30 | .. | .. | 5 50 | .. | .. | .. | .. | .. | 7 0 | 7 30 | 9 40 |
| — | **Taunton** .......... dep | 7 24 | 9 0 | .... | 10 25 | pm 12 20 | pm 2 13 | ... | 3 30 | 4 25 | 5 55 | ... | 8 45 | .. | 6 55 | 7 24 | 8 16 | 9 0 | 1020 | 1140 | pm 12 38 |
| 2 | Norton Fitzwarren .. .. | 7 30 | .. | .. | 10 29 | | 2 17 | .. | 3 34 | 4 29 | 5 59 | .. | 8 51 | .. | .. | 7 30 | 8 22 | .. | .. | .. | .. |
| 5 | Bishop's Lydeard ........ | 7 39 | 9 10 | ... | 10 37 | 12 30 | 2 24 | ... | 3 42 | 4 35 | 6 6 | ... | 8 58 | ... | 7 5 | 7 39 | 8 29 | 9 10 | 1033 | 1151 | .... |
| 9 | Crowcombe .. .. .. | 7 47 | 9 18 | .. | 10 45 | 12 37 | 2 35 | .. | 3 50 | 4 43 | 6 14 | .. | 9 5 | .. | 7 13 | 7 47 | 8 37 | 9 19 | 1042 | 12 0 | .. |
| 11¾ | Stogumber ............ | 7 53 | 9 23 | ... | 10 51 | 12 43 | 2 41 | ... | 3 56 | 4 49 | 6 21 | ... | 9 12 | ... | 7 18 | 7 53 | 8 43 | 9 25 | 1052 | 12 6 | .... |
| 15 | Williton .. .. .. .. | 8 3 | 9 33 | .. | 11 0 | 12 51 | 2 49 | .. | 4 4 | 4 57 | 6 29 | .. | 9 21 | .. | 7 26 | 8 3 | 8 53 | 9 34 | 11 2 | 1214 | .. |
| 16¾ | Watchet ............... | 8 9 | 9 39 | ... | 11 5 | 12 57 | 2 55 | ... | 4 10 | 5 4 | 6 35 | ... | 9 27 | ... | 7 31 | 8 9 | 9 0 | 9 42 | 11 9 | 1219 | .... |
| 19 | Washford .. .. .. .. | 8 17 | 9 46 | .. | 11 17 | 1 4 | 3 2 | .. | 4 18 | 5 12 | 6 42 | .. | 9 34 | .. | 7 38 | 8 17 | 9 7 | 9 49 | 1116 | 1226 | .. |
| 21¼ | Blue Anchor ............ | 8 22 | 9 51 | ... | 11 22 | 1 9 | 3 7 | ... | 4 23 | 5 17 | 6 47 | ... | 9 39 | ... | 7 45 | 8 22 | 9 13 | 9 55 | 1121 | 1233 | .... |
| 23 | Dunster .. .. .. .. | 8 27 | 9 56 | .. | 11 27 | 1 14 | 3 12 | .. | 4 28 | 5 22 | 6 52 | .. | 9 44 | .. | 7 50 | 8 26 | 9 22 | 10 0 | 1126 | 1240 | .. |
| 24¾ | **Minehead** ......... arr | 8 32 | 10 1 | .... | 11 32 | 1 19 | 3 18 | ... | 4 35 | 5 27 | 6 57 | ... | 9 50 | ... | 7 55 | 8 32 | 9 27 | 10 5 | 1131 | 1245 | 1 40 |

| | SATURDAYS—*continued* | | | | | | | | | | SUNDAYS | | | | | | | | | | | |
|---|---|---|---|---|---|---|---|---|---|---|---|---|---|---|---|---|---|---|---|---|---|---|
| | pm | am T | pm | noon X | pm | pm | pm | pm | | | am | | am | | pm | | am | | pm | | pm | |
| 61 London (Pad.) 62 .. dep | .. | 1130 | .. | 12 0 | 1 30 | 3 30 | 5 50 | 6K30 | .. | .. | .. | .. | .. | .. | .. | .. | 11 0 | .. | 1 30 | .. | 3 30 | .. |
| **Taunton** ............ dep | 1 5 | pm 2 18 | 2 55 | 3 25 | 4 45 | 6 15 | 8 45 | 1025 | .... | .... | 8 50 | .... | 1150 | .... | 1 15 | .... | pm 2 40 | .... | 4 45 | .... | 6 55 | .... |
| Norton Fitzwarren .. .. | 1 11 | .. | 2 59 | .. | 4 49 | 6 19 | 8 51 | .. | .. | .. | 8 54 | .. | .. | .. | 1 19 | .. | 2 47 | .. | 4 49 | .. | 6 59 | .. |
| Bishop's Lydeard ........ | 1 20 | .... | 3 6 | .... | 4 57 | 6 26 | 8 58 | 1036 | .... | .... | 9 0 | .... | 12 0 | .... | 1 26 | .... | 2 53 | .... | 4 55 | .... | 7 5 | .... |
| Crowcombe .. .. .. | 1 29 | .. | 3 15 | 3 48 | 5 6 | 6 34 | 9 5 | 1044 | .. | .. | 9 8 | .. | 12 8 | .. | 1 35 | .. | 3 1 | .. | 5 3 | .. | 7 13 | .. |
| Stogumber ............ | 1 35 | .... | 3 21 | .... | 5 12 | 6 40 | 9 12 | .... | .... | .... | 9 14 | .... | 1214 | .... | 1 42 | .... | 3 7 | .... | 5 9 | .... | 7 20 | .... |
| Williton .. .. .. .. | 1 44 | 2 55 | 3 32 | 4 5 | 5 21 | 6 48 | 9 21 | 11 0 | .. | .. | 9 23 | .. | 1223 | .. | 1 52 | .. | 3 16 | .. | 5 18 | .. | 7 29 | .. |
| Watchet ............... | 1 51 | .... | 3 39 | 4 11 | 5 26 | 6 55 | 9 27 | 11 5 | .... | .... | 9 28 | .... | 1228 | .... | 1 58 | .... | 3 21 | .... | 5 23 | .... | 7 34 | .... |
| Washford .. .. .. | 2 2 | .. | 3 46 | 4 19 | 5 34 | 7 2 | 9 34 | 1111 | .. | .. | 9 35 | .. | 1235 | .. | 2 5 | .. | 3 36 | .. | 5 35 | .. | 7 41 | .. |
| Blue Anchor ............ | 2 7 | .... | 3 53 | 4 32 | 5 40 | 7 7 | 9 39 | 1116 | .... | .... | 9 40 | .... | 1240 | .... | 2 10 | .... | 3 41 | .... | 5 40 | .... | 7 46 | .... |
| Dunster .. .. .. .. | 2 14 | .. | 4 0 | 4 38 | 5 47 | 7 14 | 9 44 | 1121 | .. | .. | 9 45 | .. | 1245 | .. | 2 15 | .. | 3 46 | .. | 5 45 | .. | 7 51 | .. |
| **Minehead** ......... arr | 2 20 | 3 20 | 4 5 | 4 43 | 5 52 | 7 20 | 9 50 | 1125 | .... | .... | 9 50 | .... | 1250 | .... | 2 20 | .... | 3 51 | .... | 5 50 | .... | 7 56 | .... |

| Miles | | MONDAYS TO FRIDAYS | | | | | | | | | | | | | SATURDAYS | | | | | | |
|---|---|---|---|---|---|---|---|---|---|---|---|---|---|---|---|---|---|---|---|---|---|
| | | am | am | am | | pm | | pm | pm | pm | pm | | pm | | am | am | am | am | am T | am Z | pm W |
| — | **Minehead** .. .. .. dep | 7 35 | 9 5 | 10 50 | .. | 12 20 | .. | 1 50 | 4 30 | 5 5 | 6 0 | .. | 8 5 | .. | 7 35 | 8 25 | 9 5 | 10 5 | 1040 | 1155 | 1220 |
| 1¾ | Dunster ................ | 7 39 | 9 9 | 10 54 | ... | 12 24 | ... | 1 54 | 4 34 | 5 10 | 6 4 | ... | 8 9 | ... | 7 39 | 8 29 | 9 10 | 10 11 | .... | 12 0 | 1225 |
| 3½ | Blue Anchor .. .. .. | 7 44 | 9 14 | 10 59 | .. | 12 29 | .. | 1 59 | 4 39 | 5 15 | 6 9 | .. | 8 14 | .. | 7 44 | 8 34 | 9 16 | 10 17 | .. | 12 6 | 1232 |
| 5¾ | Washford .............. | 7 50 | 9 20 | 11 5 | ... | 12 35 | ... | 2 5 | 4 45 | 5 20 | 6 15 | ... | 8 20 | ... | 7 50 | 8 40 | 9 22 | 10 24 | ... | 1214 | 1238 |
| 8 | Watchet .. .. .. .. | 7 56 | 9 26 | 11 12 | .. | 12 41 | .. | 2 13 | 4 51 | 5 32 | 6 21 | .. | 8 26 | .. | 7 56 | 8 46 | 9 29 | 10 31 | .. | 1225 | 1244 |
| 9¾ | Williton ................ | 8 3 | 9 32 | 11 19 | ... | 12 48 | ... | 2 19 | 4 57 | 5 40 | 6 27 | ... | 8 33 | ... | 8 3 | 8 52 | 9 36 | 10 38 | ... | 1232 | 1250 |
| 13 | Stogumber .. .. .. .. | 8 10 | 9 40 | 11 26 | .. | 12 57 | .. | 2 26 | 5 4 | 5 47 | 6 37 | .. | 8 40 | .. | 8 10 | .. | 9 43 | 10 45 | .. | 1239 | 1258 |
| 15¾ | Crowcombe ............ | 8 17 | 9 47 | 11 32 | ... | 1 3 | ... | 2 34 | 5 10 | 5 54 | 6 44 | ... | 8 47 | ... | 8 17 | .... | 9 50 | 10 54 | .... | 1246 | 1 5 |
| 19¾ | Bishop's Lydeard .. .. | 8 24 | 9 54 | 11 40 | .. | 1 11 | .. | 2 42 | 5 18 | 6 2 | 6 52 | .. | 8 55 | .. | 8 24 | .. | 9 59 | 11 3 | .. | 1254 | 1 13 |
| 22¾ | Norton Fitzwarren ...... | 8 30 | 10 0 | 11 46 | .... | .... | ... | 2 48 | 5 24 | 6 8 | 6 58 | ... | 9 1 | ... | 8 30 | .... | 10 6 | 11 10 | .... | .... | .... |
| 24¾ | **Taunton** .. .. .. arr | 8 35 | 10 5 | 11 51 | .. | 1 23 | .. | 2 53 | 5 38 | 6 17 | 7 3 | .. | 9 6 | .. | 8 35 | 9 20 | 10 11 | 11 19 | 1140 | 1 10 | 1 26 |
| 167¾ | 61 London (Pad.) 62 .. arr | pm 12 10 | pm 1 25 | pm 2 50 | ... | 5C33 | ... | 6G15 | 9 5 | .... | .... | .... | .... | .... | .... | pm 12 10 | pm 1P20 | .... | pm 2 40 | .... | 5 15 |

| | SATURDAYS—*continued* | | | | | | | | | | | SUNDAYS | | | | | | | | | | | |
|---|---|---|---|---|---|---|---|---|---|---|---|---|---|---|---|---|---|---|---|---|---|---|---|
| | pm | pm T | pm | pm | pm | pm | pm | pm | pm | | | am | | pm | | pm | | pm | | pm | | pm | |
| **Minehead** .. .. .. dep | 1 35 | 2 15 | 3 0 | 4 20 | 5 5 | 5 50 | 6 35 | 7 50 | 10 5 | .. | .. | 1010 | .. | 1 40 | .. | 3 10 | .. | 5 10 | .. | 6 30 | .. | 8 25 | .. |
| Dunster ................ | 1 39 | .... | 3 4 | 4 24 | 5 10 | 5 54 | 6 40 | 7 54 | 10 9 | .... | .... | 1014 | .... | 1 44 | .... | 3 14 | .... | 5 14 | .... | 6 34 | .... | 8 29 | .... |
| Blue Anchor .. .. .. | 1 45 | .. | 3 12 | 4 30 | 5 16 | 6 0 | 6 46 | 7 59 | 1014 | .. | .. | 1019 | .. | 1 49 | .. | 3 19 | .. | 5 19 | .. | 6 39 | .. | 8 34 | .. |
| Washford .............. | 1 51 | .... | 3 18 | 4 37 | 5 22 | 6 6 | 6 52 | 8 5 | 1020 | .... | .... | 1025 | .... | 1 55 | .... | 3 25 | .... | 5 25 | .... | 6 45 | .... | 8 40 | .... |
| Watchet .. .. .. .. | 1 57 | .. | 3 24 | 4 44 | 5 33 | 6 12 | 7 2 | 8 11 | 1026 | .. | .. | 1031 | .. | 2 5 | .. | 3 31 | .. | 5 31 | .. | 6 51 | .. | 8 46 | .. |
| Williton ................ | 2 4 | .... | 3 31 | 4 50 | 5 40 | 6 19 | 7 9 | 8 17 | 1033 | .... | .... | 1038 | .... | 2 12 | .... | 3 38 | .... | 5 38 | .... | 6 58 | .... | 8 53 | .... |
| Stogumber .. .. .. .. | 2 11 | .. | 3 40 | 4 58 | 5 48 | 6 26 | 7 16 | 8 25 | .. | .. | .. | 1045 | .. | 2 19 | .. | 3 45 | .. | 5 45 | .. | 7 5 | .. | 9 0 | .. |
| Crowcombe ............ | 2 19 | .... | 3 48 | 5 7 | 5 55 | 6 35 | 7 23 | 8 32 | 1047 | .... | .... | 1052 | .... | 2 26 | .... | 3 52 | .... | 5 52 | .... | 7 14 | .... | 9 7 | .... |
| Bishop's Lydeard .. .. | 2 27 | .. | 3 57 | 5 17 | 6 3 | 6 43 | 7 31 | 8 40 | 1055 | .. | .. | 11 0 | .. | 2 34 | .. | 4 0 | .. | 6 0 | .. | 7 23 | .. | 9 15 | .. |
| Norton Fitzwarren ...... | 2 33 | .... | 4 4 | 5 24 | 6 9 | 6 49 | 7 37 | 8 46 | .... | .... | .... | .... | .... | 2 40 | .... | 4 6 | .... | 6 6 | .... | 7 29 | .... | 9 21 | .... |
| **Taunton** .. .. .. arr | 2 42 | 3 20 | 4 15 | 5 32 | 6 18 | 6 55 | 7 42 | 8 51 | 11 5 | .. | .. | 1110 | .. | 2 45 | .. | 4 11 | .. | 6 15 | .. | 7 35 | .. | 9 26 | .. |
| 61 London (Pad.) 62 .. arr | .... | 6 25 | .... | 9 5 | 9 20 | .... | .... | .... | .... | .... | .... | pm 3 45 | .... | .... | .... | 7 20 | .... | 9 25 | .... | .... | .... | am 3 25 | .... |

C Via Bristol (Table 61). On Fridays arr 5 43 pm
G Limited accommodation from Bristol (Table 61)
K Via Bristol (Table 61)
P Through Carriages Minehead to Paddington 24th June to 26th August inclusive only. On 17th June, 2nd and 9th September only arr 1 42 pm
T Through Train between Paddington and Minehead
W Through Carriages Minehead to Wolverhampton (L.L.) (Table 31)
X Through Carriages Wolverhampton (L.L.) to Minehead (Table 31) until 2nd September inclusive
Z Through Train Minehead to Bristol and Paddington (arr 5 43 pm)

**A limited Road Motor Service is operated by the Western National Omnibus Company between Minehead, Porlock Village and Lynmouth**

**For OTHER TRAINS between Taunton and Norton Fitzwarren, see Tables 81 and 86**

## Table 86 TAUNTON, DULVERTON, BARNSTAPLE JUNCTION and ILFRACOMBE

**WEEK DAYS ONLY**

| Miles | | MONDAYS TO FRIDAYS | | | | | | | | SATURDAYS | | | | | | | | | | | |
|---|---|---|---|---|---|---|---|---|---|---|---|---|---|---|---|---|---|---|---|---|---|
| | | am | am | am | pm | pm | pm | pm | | pm T | am C | am T | am T | am A | am T | pm | am K | noon X | pm T | pm | pm |
| | 61 London (Pad.) 62 dep | .. | 9 30 | 11 30 | .. | 1 30 | .. | 5 50 | .. | 11F50 | .. | .. | .. | 7 0 | 9 40 | .. | 1130 | 12 0 | 1 30 | 3 30 | 5 50 |
| — | **Taunton** ........ dep | 8 5 | pm 12 15 | pm 2 33 | .... | 4 35 | 5 45 | 8 40 | .... | am 5 20 | 6 20 | 7 0 | 8 30 | 1025 | pm 12 50 | 1 48 | pm 2 25 | pm 3 35 | 4 35 | 6 15 | 8 40 |
| 2 | Norton Fitzwarren .. | .. | 12 19 | .. | .. | 4 39 | 5 49 | .. | .. | .. | .. | .. | 8 34 | 1029 | .. | .. | .. | .. | .. | 6 22 | .. |
| 6½ | Milverton ............ | 8 17 | 12 27 | 2 49 | .... | 4 47 | 5 58 | 8 54 | .... | .... | .... | 7 12 | 8 43 | 1038 | 1 4 | 2 2 | .... | .... | 4 47 | 6 30 | 8 54 |
| 9½ | Wiveliscombe.. .. .. | 8 25 | 12 34 | 2 56 | .. | 4 54 | 6 5 | 9 0 | .. | 5 40 | 6 39 | 7 18 | 8 51 | 1046 | 1 14 | 2 10 | 2 47 | .. | 4 54 | 6 37 | 9 0 |
| 14½ | Venn Cross ........... | 8 36 | 12 45 | 3 7 | .... | 5 5 | 6 17 | 9 11 | .... | .... | .... | 7 29 | 9 4 | .... | 1 27 | .... | .... | .... | 5 5 | 6 48 | 9 11 |
| 17¾ | Morebath.. .. .. .. | 8 42 | 12 51 | 3 13 | .. | 5 12 | 6 24 | 9 16 | .. | .. | .. | 7 36 | 9 10 | .. | 1 34 | .. | .. | .. | 5 10 | 6 54 | 9 16 |
| 19¼ | Morebath Junction Halt | 8 47 | 12 56 | 3 19 | .... | 5 19 | 6 30 | 9 21 | .... | .... | .... | .... | 9 15 | .... | .... | .... | .... | .... | .. | 6 59 | 9 21 |
| 21 | Dulverton .. .. .. | 8 53 | 1 2 | 3 27 | .. | 5 26 | 6 35 | 9 29 | .. | 6 9 | 7 5 | 7 45 | 9 21 | 1118 | 1 50 | 2 37 | 3 18 | 4 23 | 5 26 | 7 7 | 9 29 |
| 24¾ | East Anstey .......... | 9 3 | 1 11 | 3 38 | .... | 5 36 | 6 49 | 9 38 | .... | .... | .... | 7 56 | 9 30 | 1128 | 2 5 | 2 48 | .... | .... | 5 36 | 7 16 | 9 38 |
| 26½ | Yeo Mill Halt.. .. .. | 9 8 | 1 15 | 3 43 | .. | 5 41 | 6 54 | 9 43 | .. | .. | .. | .. | 9 35 | .. | 2 13 | .. | .. | .. | .. | 7 20 | 9 43 |
| 30 | Bishop's Nympton and | 9 14 | 1 21 | 3 49 | .... | 5 47 | 7 1 | 9 49 | .... | .... | 7 25 | 8 6 | 9 41 | 1139 | 2 20 | 2 58 | .... | .... | 5 47 | 7 26 | 9 49 |
| 34¼ | South Molton [Molland | 9 23 | 1 29 | 3 57 | .. | 5 56 | 7b18 | 9 58 | .. | 6 38 | 7 38 | 8 18 | 9 55 | 1147 | 2 28 | 3 6 | 3 46 | 5 0 | 6 0 | 7 34 | 9 58 |
| 37½ | Filleigh ............... | 9 32 | 1 39 | 4 7 | .... | 6 4 | 7 27 | 10 7 | .... | .... | .... | 8 28 | 10 6 | 1156 | 2 38 | 3 16 | .... | .... | 6 15 | 7 45 | 10 7 |
| 40¾ | Swimbridge .. .. .. | 9 39 | 1 45 | 4 13 | .. | 6 11 | 7 34 | 10 14 | .. | .. | .. | 8 35 | 1020 | 12 5 | 2 48 | 3 25 | .. | .. | 6 24 | 7 52 | 1014 |
| 45¼ | **Barnstaple Junction** arr | 9 49 | 1 55 | 4 23 | .... | 6 21 | 7 44 | 10 24 | .... | 7 5 | 8 8 | 8 45 | 1033 | 1216 | 3 0 | 3 36 | 4 18 | 5 34 | 6 37 | 8 2 | 1024 |
| 60¾ | **Ilfracombe** .. arr | 10 52 | 3 42 | 5 56 | .. | 7 6 | 9 6 | 11F52 | .. | 7 58 | 9 4 | 9 42 | 1122 | 1 40 | 3 56 | 4 38 | 5 10 | 6 35 | 7 37 | 9 6 | .. |

| Miles | | MONDAYS TO FRIDAYS | | | | | | | | | SATURDAYS | | | | | | | | | | | | |
|---|---|---|---|---|---|---|---|---|---|---|---|---|---|---|---|---|---|---|---|---|---|---|---|
| | | am | am | am | | pm | | pm | pm | | am | am | am M | am N | am L | am P | noon Z | pm K | pm | pm | pm T | pm T | pm W |
| — | **Ilfracombe** .. .. dep | .. | 6 50 | 8 55 | .. | 1220 | .. | 3 0 | 5 57 | .. | .. | 6 50 | 8 30 | 9 22 | 1010 | 11 0 | 12 0 | 1225 | 2 55 | .. | 5 10 | 6 37 | 8 5 |
| 15 | **Barnstaple Junction** dp | 6 42 | 8 12 | 10 2 | .... | 1 17 | .... | 4 0 | 6 47 | .... | 6 42 | 7 45 | 9 18 | 10 6 | 11 5 | 1152 | 1248 | 1 10 | 3 55 | 5 0 | 5 53 | 7 20 | 8 48 |
| 20 | Swimbridge .. .. | 6 52 | 8 22 | 1013 | .. | 1 27 | .. | 4 14 | 6 57 | .. | 6 56 | 8 3 | .. | 1024 | 1121 | .. | 1 0 | 1 24 | 4 8 | .. | 6 7 | 7 35 | .. |
| 23¼ | Filleigh ............... | 7 1 | 8 30 | 1021 | .... | 1 38 | .... | 4 22 | 7 5 | .... | 7 4 | 8 10 | .... | 1033 | 1131 | .... | 1 8 | .... | 4 18 | .... | 6 18 | 7 44 | .... |
| 26½ | South Molton [Molland | 7 13 | 8 42 | 1033 | .. | 1 49 | .. | 4 34 | 7 17 | .. | 7 12 | 8 18 | 9 50 | 1048 | 1148 | 1220 | 1 16 | 1 41 | 4 34 | 5 39 | 6 27 | 7 53 | 9 16 |
| 30¾ | Bishop's Nympton and | 7 21 | 8 50 | 1041 | .... | 1 57 | .... | 4 42 | 7 25 | .... | 7 24 | 8 26 | .... | 1056 | 1158 | .... | 1 24 | 1 50 | 4 53 | 5 48 | 6 36 | 8 1 | .... |
| 34¼ | Yeo Mill Halt .. .. | 7 28 | 8 57 | 1048 | .. | 2 4 | .. | 4 49 | 7 32 | .. | 7 31 | 8 33 | .. | 11 4 | 12 5 | .. | .. | .. | .. | .. | 6 43 | 8 8 | .. |
| 36 | East Anstey .......... | 7 34 | 9 3 | 1053 | .... | 2 9 | .... | 4 54 | 7 37 | .... | 7 36 | 8 38 | .... | 1110 | 1210 | .... | 1 35 | .... | 5 5 | .... | 6 49 | 8 13 | .... |
| 39¾ | Dulverton .. .. .. | 7 43 | 9 15 | 11 2 | .. | 2 15 | .. | 5 3 | 7 47 | .. | 7 45 | 8 47 | 1016 | 1120 | 1220 | 1245 | 1 43 | 2 18 | 5 14 | 6 9 | 7 3 | 8 26 | 9 47 |
| 41½ | Morebath Junction Halt | 7 48 | 9 20 | 11 8 | .... | 2 21 | .... | 5 9 | 7 52 | .... | 7 51 | 8 52 | .... | 1126 | 1225 | .... | .... | .... | 5 19 | .... | 7 9 | 8 34 | .... |
| 43 | Morebath .. .. .. | 7 52 | 9 24 | 1111 | .. | 2 25 | .. | 5 13 | 7 56 | .. | 7 54 | 8 55 | .. | 1130 | 1229 | .. | .. | .. | 5 23 | .. | 7 12 | 8 38 | .. |
| 46½ | Venn Cross ........... | 8 0 | 9 32 | 1119 | .... | 2 33 | .... | 5 21 | 8 4 | .... | 8 2 | 9 3 | .... | 1138 | 1237 | .... | .... | .... | 5 31 | .... | 7 20 | 8 46 | .... |
| 51¼ | Wiveliscombe .. .. | 8 10 | 9 41 | 1129 | .. | 2 42 | .. | 5 31 | 8 14 | .. | 8 11 | 9 12 | 1045 | 1148 | 1247 | 1 12 | 2 10 | 2 48 | 5 41 | 6 38 | 7 32 | 9 0 | 1013 |
| 54¼ | Milverton ............ | 8 16 | 9 47 | 1135 | .... | 2 47 | .... | 5 37 | 8 21 | .... | 8 17 | 9 18 | .... | 1154 | 1253 | .... | 2 16 | .... | 5 47 | .... | 7 38 | 9 7 | .... |
| 58¾ | Norton Fitzwarren .. | 8 24 | 9 55 | .. | .. | .. | .. | .. | 8 30 | .. | 8 25 | .. | .. | 12 2 | 1 1 | .. | .. | .. | 5 55 | .. | 7 46 | 9 15 | .. |
| 60¾ | **Taunton** ......... arr | 8 30 | 10 0 | 1148 | .... | 3 0 | .... | 5 51 | 8 36 | .... | 8 30 | 9 36 | 11 3 | 1210 | 1 6 | 1 30 | 2 30 | 3 7 | 6 1 | 6 55 | 7 51 | 9 21 | 1030 |
| 203¾ | 61 London (Pad.) 62 arr | pm 12 10 | pm 1 25 | pm 2 50 | .. | 6G15 | .. | 9 5 | .. | .. | pm 12 10 | pm 1Y42 | pm 2 40 | .. | .. | 5 15 | .. | 6 25 | 9 5 | .. | .. | .. | .. |

A Through Train Taunton to Torrington arr 1 3 pm
*b* Arr 7 9 pm
C Runs 22nd July to 2nd September inclusive only. Through Train between Taunton and Ilfracombe
F Friday nights
G Limited accommodation from Bristol (Table 61)
K Through Carriages between Paddington and Ilfracombe
L Runs 22nd July to 2nd September. Through Train Ilfracombe to Taunton. From 5th August to 2nd September, Through Carriages to Wolverhampton (L.L.)
M Through Train Ilfracombe to Bristol. Commencing 1st July extended to Manchester (Ex.) (Tables 61 and 168)
N Through Train Ilfracombe to Taunton. Commencing 24th June extended to Cardiff (Tables 61 and 104)
P Through Carriages Ilfracombe to Wolverhampton (L.L.) (Table 31)
T Through Train between Taunton and Ilfracombe
Y From 24th June to 26th August arr 1 20 pm
W Will not run after 2nd September. Through Train Ilfracombe to Taunton
X Will not run after 2nd September. Through Carriages Wolverhampton (L.L.) to Ilfracombe (Table 31)
Z Through Train Torrington dep 11 48 am and Bideford dep 11 58 am to Taunton

**A Road Motor Service is operated by the Southern National Omnibus Company between Barnstaple Junction and Chelfham Cross, Bratton Fleming, Blackmoor Gate, Parracombe, Woody Bay Cross and Lynton**

**For OTHER TRAINS between Taunton and Norton Fitzwarren, see Tables 81 and 82—Morebath Junction Halt and Dulverton, Table 87**

*Wellington* at Wellington! 'Castle' No. 5074 *Wellington* races through the station with the 'up' *Torbay Express* on 6 July 1957. The layout at Wellington, as with the other significant intermediate stations to Exeter, can be seen here as it was intended.   *R. C. Riley*

'Modified Hall', No. 7925, *Westol Hall,* roars through Tiverton Junction on its way to the summit of the Devon-Somerset border at Whiteball Tunnel with the 8.30 a.m. Penzance-Swansea on 5 August 1957. Tiverton Junction was rebuilt in 1932 as part of the GWR programme of modernisation in the West of England. All principal stations between Taunton and Exeter had through lines as shown here.   *P.Gray*

In November 1935 the company announced an ambitious plan of works to improve and promote services. Whilst it was by no means focused entirely upon the West Country, a great deal of work was envisaged therein. As with the earlier developments, the new works would be carried out with government support, the Treasury releasing funds at low rates of interest. The work would obviously enhance the image and performance of the GWR, but was also encouraged as a purposeful means of providing employment in otherwise difficult times. The programme for the West of England included: a by-pass line between Dawlish Warren and Newton Abbot, a fly-over scheme at Exeter St Davids for Southern Railway services, a new direct line from St Germans to Looe, in Cornwall, upgrading of both the Barnstaple and Minehead branches with a view to tourist traffic, likewise, the Newquay branch in Cornwall, together with extensive rebuilding and modernisation at Paignton, Plymouth North Road, Newquay and Penzance stations, and at Millbay Docks, where passenger facilities were to be improved.

The new route proposed between Dawlish Warren to a point east of Newton Abbot station, at the head of the Teign estuary, was part of the larger project including the work in the Taunton area and at the station westward through Exeter to Exminster. With the new line there would be much less pressure and congestion on the coastal section between Exeter and Newton Abbot allowing all those services not required to call at Teignmouth and Dawlish to proceed at greater speed inland. The new line would also remove the problems of dislocation and restriction of services along the sea-wall section during winter time with damage inflicted by the sea and from landslips from the treacherous red sandstone cliffs along that route.

Plans for the new route entailed a double-track section of 8½ miles. Leaving the original main line north of Dawlish Warren, the new route would curve westward climbing for three miles on a gradient of 1 in 50 on a section requiring considerable cuttings and embankments together with a tunnel almost 3/4 mile long. The central section of just under two miles was to have a gradient of 1 in 617, but required a long tunnel running for the greater part of this entire section. The western descent towards Newton Abbot began on a gradient of 1 in 150, again calling for considerable earthworks and two short tunnels. This section of just under 2½ miles led to the final one mile section on a gradient of 1 in 33⁰, rejoining the original main line at the head of the Teign estuary. Had it been built it would have played a more valuable, but much less aesthetic, role than the coastal route; the problems of damage to the sea-wall section are still very much with us today. Preparatory work was carried out in connection with this scheme but costs, time and the onset of war prevented any real progress.

Whilst the sea-wall section between Dawlish Warren and Teignmouth contributed to congestion, the situation at Exeter St Davids was critical. GWR and Southern trains crossed each other's path at St Davids and shared the tracks northward to the Southern's own territory at Cowley Bridge Junction. The growth in general traffic was in itself sufficient to cause concern, but with the heavy demand from both companies in connection with summer tourist trains, the existing provision was woefully inadequate.

Under the proposals by the Great Western, and subject to agreement from the Southern Railway, it was the intention to build a fly-over section, complete with station facilities for Southern services. From the west end of St. Davids Tunnel the elevated section would curve across the GWR lines giving access to a new island platform for the exclusive use of Southern trains at a point west of the Great Western station. The platforms were intended to be 850 feet in length. Thereafter, the Southern lines would continue eastward over the GWR yard on their own tracks to Cowley Bridge. With Southern traffic provided for in this way the GWR could extend and modernise its facilities, the plans being to remodel and extend the platforms, to replace the level crossing immediately north of the station with a bridge – this being the responsibility of the City authorities – and to provide a new goods yard north of the station on the 'up' west side. Of these fascinating plans only the goods yard actually materialised, and this was the result of wartime demands, not the scheme envisaged by the GWR. Exeter's 'Riverside' Yard opened in the dark days of October 1943.

Torbay, as the premier holiday area, was bound to feature in Great Western plans. Paignton station was in need of considerable enlargement given the restricted site, the popularity of the resort and the intensive summer service to Torbay. Steps were taken during the twenties to develop facilities. Torre, Torquay and Paignton were all provided with two-way working at the platforms to allow for easier, more flexible movements between 1925 and 1927. Platforms were lengthened and in 1928 work began to double the line between Paignton and Goodrington. Goodrington Halt was opened in July 1928 as a single platform, it was renamed Goodrington Sands in 1929, and was enlarged by the provision of another platform when the line was doubled and extended through the station in May 1930. The platforms at Paignton were extended southward, especially the 'down' side, at the same time with considerable extra siding space being provided alongside the down platform. When the new goods shed for the Paignton district was opened in June 1931, west of the line between Paignton and Goodrington, more land was freed at the station. The old goods shed was on the west, 'up' side of the station.

The Development (Loan Guarantee and Grants) Act of 1929, was responsible for the works outlined above and six years later more ambitious plans were tabled for Paignton under the GWR (Additional Powers) Act, 1936. It was proposed to develop a greatly enlarged station with five platforms. Much additional land would be required to the west and to the south of the station. New station buildings were scheduled for the 'up' side. Given the need to extend southward, the plans involved the closure of Sands Road level crossing, which, together with that serving Torbay Road immediately north of the station, effectively enclosed the site. The Dartmouth Road crossing was to be widened and a subway constructed for pedestrians to cross the line. Sands Road crossing would become part of the new station site with a subway being provided for pedestrians, but it was eventually agreed that a road bridge at Sands Road would be the best course. At Goodrington, the crossing immediately north of the station was to be replaced by a bridge, and new sidings and a turntable were to be set out west of the line, alongside the station. The scheme, overall, was approved and would complement the investment on the part of the town at Goodrington in

connection with the park and sea-front development. Both the town and the GWR were anxious to promote Paignton both as a resort and a residential centre but whilst both parties looked to a positive future with important preparatory works being well under way, the scheme was halted in 1939 with the outbreak of war. The post-war period saw the completion of the work planned for Goodrington, but this, in its final form, was not done until as late as 1957. Paignton did not get its new station and had to make do with its cramped conditions and restrictive level crossings for the post-war years, the period of peak holiday traffic.

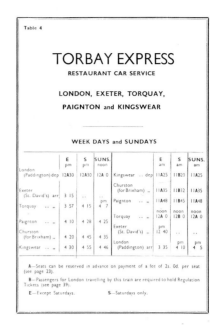

Table 4

## TORBAY EXPRESS
### RESTAURANT CAR SERVICE

#### LONDON, EXETER, TORQUAY, PAIGNTON and KINGSWEAR

**WEEK DAYS and SUNDAYS**

| | E pm | S pm | SUNS. noon | | E am | S am | SUNS. am |
|---|---|---|---|---|---|---|---|
| London (Paddington) dep | 12A30 | 12A30 | 12A 0 | Kingswear .. dep | 11A25 | 11B20 | 11A25 |
| | | | | Churston (for Brixham) .. | 11A35 | 11B32 | 11A35 |
| Exeter (St. David's) arr | 3 15 | .. | .. pm | Paignton .. .. | 11A48 | 11B45 | 11A48 |
| Torquay .. .. | 3 57 | 4 15 | 4 7 | | noon | noon | noon |
| | | | | Torquay .. .. | 12B 0 | 12B 0 | 12A 0 |
| Paignton .. .. | 4 10 | 4 28 | 4 25 | Exeter (St. David's) .. | pm 12 40 | .. | .. |
| Churston (for Brixham) .. | 4 20 | 4 45 | 4 35 | London (Paddington) arr | 3 35 | pm 4 10 | pm 4 5 |
| Kingswear .. .. | 4 30 | 4 55 | 4 46 | | | | |

A—Seats can be reserved in advance on payment of a fee of 2s. 0d. per seat (see page 23).

B—Passengers for London travelling by this train are required to hold Regulation Tickets (see page 39).

E—Except Saturdays.        S—Saturdays only.

*Opposite top:*
With safety valves roaring 'Castle' No. 5071 *Spitfire* runs the sea-wall between Dawlish and Teignmouth with the 'down' *Cornishman*, on 19 July 1956. Note the large number of people at the windows making the most of this shore-line spectacle.        *R. C. Riley*

*Opposite bottom:*
'Castle' No. 5055, *Earl of Eldon* takes the 'up' *Devonian* away from Teignmouth station on 17 July 1958. The 'down' platform , seen here, was considerably extended in 1938, reflecting Teignmouth's popularity as a resort. The train is about to begin its run along the famous sea-wall section.        *R. C. Riley*

*Below:*
*The Torbay Express* hurries past Teignmouth Old Quay Signal Box on its way westward, 14 July 1958, headed by 'Castle' No. 5034, *Corfe Castle*.        *R. C. Riley*

*Left:*
A Sunday excursion for the coast passes Cowley Bridge Junction on 14 June 1959 with 'King' No. 6021 *King Richard II* in charge. The ex-Southern Railway route to Plymouth, North Devon and North Cornwall can also be seen here.

*M. Mensing*

*Below:* The loop lines provided for platforms at most intermediate stations between Taunton and Exeter during the early thirties are shown to good effect here at Stoke Canon on 6 July 1957. 'Hall' No. 5999, *Wollaton Hall*, pilots 'Grange' No. 6830 *Buckenhill Grange* on a heavy eastbound return holiday train. Stoke Canon was the junction for the delightful Exe Valley line.

*R. C. Riley*

Plymouth was, eventually, to fare better than Paignton. Rebuilding at Plymouth began early in 1938 with some preparatory work in the previous year. Houndiscombe Road Bridge between North Road and Mutley was replaced during 1938, the new, reinforced concrete structure bridging a four-track cutting with a much widened roadway giving 45 feet between the parapets. The former masonry arch bridge crossed double track with only 22 feet between the parapets. Quadrupling through Mutley to Laira had been intended at the turn of the century but the 1938 plan was to provide extra sidings alongside the main line that were to extend on the 'up' side, to the site of Mutley Station, closed 3 July 1939. (Millbay closed not long after, on 23 April 1941).

West of the station, considerable work was carried out, widening the embankment and the bridge over Saltash Road. Five massive girders were required for this new bridge, these being up to 113 feet long by 7 feet 1½ inches deep, and weighing over 72 tons 5cwt. As part of this programme to lay quadruple track across the bridge, Plymouth North Road's West Signal Box had to be re-sited immediately north of its original site, at the edge of the new embankment. The West box was moved

in late January 1938 and by the end of the year it was recorded that the new platforms No. 7 and 8 were in use; platforms No. 5 and 6 were promised for the following summer. These works – the platforms being over 1,000 feet long and incorporating new waiting rooms, refreshment room etc – saw the 'up' side assume the proportions of a modern, progressive station. Further work was halted by the outbreak of war, but was resumed from the mid-fifties as the photographs show.

The work was completed in stages by the early sixties; with Dr Beeching officially opening the station on 26 March 1962. Three extensive island platforms connected by subways, and a new entrance, booking hall, waiting rooms and refreshment rooms with the ten-storey administrative block embodied all that was considered modern and desirable in the early sixties. The station entrance was on the 'down' side being convenient for the city. A new power signal box, immediately west of the station on the 'down' side provided for multiple-aspect coloured light signalling and controlled the system from Laira Junction in the east to Keyham in the west. It also meant the closure of six manual boxes, including North Road, East and West, the former dating from the initial modernisation of 1938.

Rebuilding work on the west end, 'down side'. 'Grange' No. 6826, *Nannerth Grange* stands at platform 3 with a ballast train, 8 April, 1960. This, and the photograph overleaf taken from much the same point allow for useful comparisons and contrasts.    *R. C. Riley*

*Plymouth* at Plymouth: an interesting photograph from August 1947. Southern Railway Light Pacific No. 21C103, *Plymouth* (later re-numbered 34003) draws into North Road from Plymouth Friary with the splendid stock of the 'up' *Devon Belle*. Obviously no GWR heritage, but the photograph illustrates clearly the final stages in the removal of the old station roof on the GWR 'down' side and the new structure replacing it was seen here to the left. A valuable record of the interim stages of rebuilding; much at this stage remaining to be done.  *Roger Venning*

The view westward on the 'down' side at the west end of the station on 18 July 1956. North Road's West Box, shifted to the edge of the widened, quadrupled section on the approach to the station over Saltash Road in 1938, can be seen here.  *R. C. Riley*

64

The Kingswear branch also saw valuable developments between the Wars. The two largest projects involved a deviation inland to avoid the rebuilding of two timber viaducts, Longwood and Noss, near Kingswear, and development work in and around Kingswear Station.

Somewhat in the style of the Saltash-St Germans main line deviation of 1908, this was a more modest project over a length of 60 chains involving much excavation for cuttings and embankments. Built with provision for double-track should this ever be required the contract was let in November 1919, the work being completed in May 1923.

Development at Kingswear involved the rebuilding of Waterhead Viaduct at the entrance to the station, further reclamation of land from Waterhead Creek, east of the line, for additional sidings, a larger turntable and the extension of the platform. The viaduct was needed as a replacement, in steel, for the original wooden structure dating back to 1864; the new viaduct also carried double-track and was completed in 1928. Taken together with the installation of the new turntable, and the extension of the platform to 850 feet, completed in May 1929, the improvements reflected significant upgrading of the branch. Hookhills and Broadsands viaducts were also strengthened in 1928, and whilst replacement for the wooden viaducts at Longwood and Noss by the deviation, and the rebuilding of Waterhead Viaduct was obviously desirable by the third decade of the twentieth century, the work overall reflected the increase in traffic and trade. Tourism was an important contributory factor here and in its modified capacity to accommodate heavier locomotives and longer trains, the operational efficiency and status of the branch was substantially increased. This was perhaps best symbolised by the sight of a *King* class locomotive heading the 'up' *Torbay Express* at the platform at Kingswear, the ideal imagery of prestige and quality service to the direct advantage of the GWR and the community generally.

Having considered the Kingswear branch it would be useful at this point to look at developments and progress on the branch lines west of Taunton and their role regarding tourist traffic.

Minehead and Ilfracombe were important resorts for the GWR. Holiday traffic to and from these locations was given a distinct boost in the early 1930s when detailed work was carried out to upgrade branch line operations.

The branch from Norton Fitzwarren to Minehead was opened in two stages; the first, to Watchet, on 31 March 1862, and, finally, to Minehead on 16 July 1874. Worked by the Bristol and Exeter Railway, this broad gauge line of 22³/₄ miles was developed by two distinct companies: the West Somerset Railway from Norton Fitzwarren to Watchet, and the Minehead Railway Company from Watchet to Minehead. Stations along the line were provided at Bishops Lydeard, Crowcombe, Stogumber, Williton, Watchet, Washford, Blue Anchor and Dunster. Modest improvements were made at stations along the line in the early years of this century – loops at Bishops Lydeard, Blue Anchor and platform extensions at Minehead, Williton and Crowcombe, for example – but the most significant changes were those introduced by the Great Western between 1933 and 1937, the bulk of the work being in 1934.

Passing loops, controlled by their respective signal boxes, were provided at Leigh Bridge, between Crowcombe and Stogumber, and at Kentsford, between Watchet and Williton, in July 1933. These loops were 750 feet in length and were laid so as to allow trains to pass at speeds of up to 40 mph. Automatic token exchanges were installed. Prior to these extra loops, passing places were available only at Bishops Lydeard, Crowcombe, Williton and Blue Anchor. Working down the branch, not in chronological order, the line was doubled between Norton Fitzwarren and Bishops Lydeard in June 1936, the down loop also being extended slightly in September of that year. At Crowcombe the loop and platforms were extended in April 1934, and the platforms at Stogumber were also extended that year. The loop at Williton was lengthened in June 1937 whilst the platforms at Watchet and Washford were extended in 1934. In the same year, the loop and platforms were lengthened at Blue Anchor; likewise, in the spring of 1934, the platform was lengthened at Dunster, and the line doubled from a point immediately beyond the station at the Minehead end, into the terminus itself.

Development at Minehead was focused on two specific periods, 1905 and 1934. In the summer of 1905 the island platform was extended and a turntable was installed south of the station. The signal box was re-sited off the end of the platform extension, having previously been at an angle to the end of the original platform to the south, and immediately beyond a siding. Under the improvements of 1934 and the doubling from Dunster, the island platform was lengthened considerably and more sidings were provided again, to the south of the platform. Improved lighting and a canopy over the platform extending 200 feet from the station buildings helped to improve the rather stark appearance of the station prior to this.

Timetable comparisons over a period of thirty years show that weekday services between Taunton and Minehead were quite comparable but that Saturday and Sunday services in the early 1960s were significantly better. The number of through services and through carriages from Paddington and the Midlands reflected the popularity of the resort.

The GWR had access to Ilfracombe via the LSWR line from Barnstaple, opened on 20 July 1874, indeed Barnstaple itself was first served by the broad gauge North Devon Railway from Exeter to Crediton some time before GWR representation arrived. North Devon trains began on 1 August 1884; nine years later the LSWR leased the line, introduced mixed gauge and took complete control on 1 January 1865. The Devon and Somerset Railway Company, representing broad gauge interests and, therefore, opposed by the rival London and South Western, was incorporated in 1864 to build its line from Norton Fitzwarren to Barnstaple. The line was to be 43 miles in length, with intermediate stations, and was opened with some difficulty in two stages: to Wiveliscombe, a distance of 7¹/₂ miles, on 8 June 1871, and to Barnstaple on 1 November 1873.

Worked by the Bristol and Exeter Railway and brought into the Great Western fold in 1901, this was a difficult line to construct and operate. It involved much heavy engineering work including two substantial viaducts and three tunnels. The viaducts – Tone, east of Venn Cross, was 162 yards long and 100 feet high, and Castle Hill, near Filleigh, 232 yards long and 94 feet high – were constructed of wrought iron lattice work resting on masonry piers. Bathealton Tunnel, between

The expanse of the point rodding and the footbridge gives indication of the considerable significance of Norton Fitzwarren in times past. Under redevelopment in the early thirties, the station comprised its signal box seen here alongside the 'down' relief line; the island platform for the down relief and down main lines and the opposite, island platform, for 'up' main and up relief lines. The junctions for Minehead and Barnstaple were immediately west of the station. This view, on 6 September 1947, shows 2251 Class 0-6-0 No. 2215 leaving for Minehead.

*Roger Venning*

An unusual and revealing view of Venn Cross looking towards Barnstaple, as seen from above the entrance to Venn Cross Tunnel (246 yards). The deeply rural character of the Devon-Somerset border district is obvious here, so, also, is the nature of the station site itself. Venn Cross was a split-site arrangement, with the platforms and waiting room sin the cutting and the booking office and entrance, above, at road level. A loop was first provided in 1905 but the extended section, seen here, dates from 1937.

4300 Class 2-6-0 No. 6327 is photographed entering the station with the 10.50 a.m. Barnstaple Junction-Taunton on 3 June 1963.

*P. Gray*

Wiveliscombe and Venn Cross, was 440 yards; Venn Cross, east of the station, was 246 yards and Castle Hill, 317 yards. Taken together with the heavy gradients and the fact that over the 43 miles there were originally only three passing loops – Wiveliscombe, Dulverton and South Molton – efficiency and convenience was not a priority. Some indication of the problem with the gradients can be given by these representative examples. Beyond Milverton the line climbed for two miles on gradients between 1 in 60 and 1 in 70. Between Venn Cross and Morebath the line fell for over three miles on gradients between 1 in 60 and 1 in 66. Similarly, the climb from Dulverton to East Anstey and the descent thereafter to Bishops Nympton and the River Yeo was characterised by gradients of 1 in 58 to 1 in 70.

As with the Minehead branch, there were improvements in the late nineteenth and early twentieth centuries involving the extension of platforms and the provision of passing loops. By 1905 for example, Milverton, Venn Cross, Morebath, East Anstey, Bishops Nympton and Swimbridge had loops with 'up' and 'down' platforms, leaving Filleigh the distinction of being the only single line station. (A plan to build a line from Filleigh northward to Lynmouth, authorised in 1885, fell through leaving Lynton and Lynmouth largely to the LSWR from 1898 via the narrow gauge Lynton and Barnstaple Railway). With the opening of the Tiverton and North Devon Railway on 1 August 1884 trains began working between Tiverton and Dulverton joining the Taunton-Barnstaple line at Morebath Junction. A loop was available here and immediately west of the junction the appropriately named Morebath Junction Halt was opened on 1 December 1928. Another halt, Yeo Mill, between East Anstey and Bishops Nympton, was opened on 27 June 1932.

Well aware of the potential of Ilfracombe and North Devon generally, the Great Western invested in the line from the mid-thirties. The section from Norton Fitzwarren, on the main line, to Milverton was doubled early in 1937, and in the previous year the loop at Milverton Station was again lengthened. Other stations had their loops and, in some cases, platforms extended during 1937. Filleigh was provided with a loop as part of this programme of work. Like the Minehead line, automatic token exchanges were provided.

Until June 1887 Barnstaple was the terminus for services from Taunton. From 1 June that year a link line was opened to the LSWR at Barnstaple Junction offering the vital access on to Ilfracombe, again over extremely steep gradients. All trains from Taunton had to reverse at their Barnstaple terminus (later named Barnstaple Victoria), at least until the summer of 1905, when the installation of the east curve gave direct access to the link line. The latter was just over 1¼ miles in length, the rival companies' stations also being separated by the River Taw. A lattice work wrought iron structure of five spans carried the line across the river. The direct east curve was closed on the outbreak of World War Two, being reopened in June 1960 when the GWR terminus was closed.

The South Western's line, 14 miles and 74 chains to Ilfracombe, was extremely heavily graded and involved another crossing of the River Taw between Barnstaple junction and Barnstaple Town. From Braunton, six miles from Barnstaple Junction, the line began a gruelling ascent of some six miles to the summit at Mortehoe with long stretches as bad as 1 in 40. From Mortehoe there was a shorter but fiercer descent at 1 in 36 to the terminus at Ilfracombe, high above the town.

With the construction of the direct Westbury route in 1906, and the Westbury and Frome avoiding lines in 1933, the GWR offered the shorter route to Ilfracombe. From Paddington the distance was 203¾ miles, as against 226½ miles from Waterloo.

Whilst the Ilfracombe and Minehead lines were so important as through routes to the resorts, the branches were also valuable in themselves as tourist attractions. The Taunton-Barnstaple line, for example, ran along the southern reaches of Exmoor and the Brendon Hills. For the interested passenger, the magnificent panorama through the carriage window made for a rich and varied aesthetic experience. Lush fields, woodland, the rivers and the slopes of Exmoor itself had infinite appeal in a rural landscape, in many ways, lost to the modern world. Hikers could make use of the isolated wayside stations to gain almost immediate access to this magnificent landscape. Similarly, the Minehead line offered its delights. Crowcombe, for example, was a gateway to the Quantocks whilst Dunster presented a very different rural experience, all in their own ways reflecting the rich and varied heritage of the region.

Devon's branches offered their own equally appealing attractions. The Exe Valley line, for example, was a rural delight, so also was the Kingsbridge branch, both being aesthetic experiences in themselves. In retrospect they seem now to have been the virtual embodiment of the land of lost content where the steam train in the landscape was part of the order and fabric of life. The Moretonhampstead branch with its access to the eastern reaches of Dartmoor-Lustleigh, Bovey Tracey for Haytor and Becky Falls, was resonant of adventure and delight.

To the west, the Tavistock-Lauceston line, the Plym Valley and Yelverton for Princetown and the heart of the Moor, provided fascinating means of access to beautiful Britain. To this end, the GWR opened many halts promoting easier access to the countryside. The Tavistock and Princetown lines were particular cases in point. South of Yelverton, Plym Bridge and Shaugh Bridge halts were opened on 1 May 1906 and 19 October 1907 respectively; Whitchurch Down Platform, south of Tavistock, opened on 1 September 1906. Clearbrook Halt, an evocative name, south of Yelverton, came later, on 29 October 1928. Yelverton became the junction for the Princetown branch from 1 May 1885. Before this, the station for the Princetown line was Horrabridge, 1½ miles northward, towards Tavistock.

The isolated Princetown branch opened 11 August 1883. The tortuous line of 10½ miles from Yelverton to the terminus owed much to the former Plymouth and Dartmoor Railway, having followed its alignment. Gradients and curves defined the line, climbing the wild hills like a goat, as S P B Mais put it. The gradient profile tells its own story; likewise the circuitous route which, on paper, looks more like the plan of an early James Brindley contour canal than a railway line. General goods and passengers and traffic in granite sustained the line for many years, with tourist traffic becoming valuable in the twenties and thirties. This was most clearly reflected in the provision of three halts – Burrator opened on 18 May 1925, King Tor on 2 April 1928 and Ingra Tor, later on 2 March 1936. Dousland Station was the only intermediate stop when services commenced in 1883.

*Above:*
Clearbrook Halt, south of Yelverton on the Plymouth-Tavistock-Launceston branch. It saw useful excursion traffic like that seen here in early August 1962. Scouts watch the arrival of 4500 Class No. 4567 with its 'B Set' forming the 10.15 a.m. Launceston-Plymouth. This was the last year of operation on this branch and the attractive setting and standards of maintenance and provision for this minor location is well worth the mention. Clearbrook was opened on 29 October, 1928. *P. Gray*

*Opposite:*
Yelverton on the Plymouth-Tavistock-Launceston branch was the junction for Princetown as from 1 May 1885. The Princetown branch opened on 11 August 1883, Horrabridge being the exchange station during the interim. In this view of May 1955, a 4400 Class 2-6-2T No. 4410 stands at Yelverton on the Princetown branch platform.

*P. Q. Treloar*

Two views of the line between Ingra Tor and King Tor halts, one of a train climbing to Princetown, and one showing the descent. These views, taken in May 1955, record the last summer for services over this magnificent moorland spectacle; the line closed on 5 March, 1956. *P. Q. Treloar*

# Chapter Four
# Transatlantic Trade – Millbay Docks

An extensive survey of the history and development of Millbay Docks and the related railway involvement is outside the scope and essential focus of this work. Some indication of the part played by the docks and the GWR in promoting Trans-Atlantic liner traffic and Ocean Liner specials from Millbay to Paddington, has significance, however, as it brought the Company valuable revenue and prestige. This, of course, was often holiday traffic in the opposite direction, out of Devon, to other parts of Britain.

Since the early years of this century the GWR had targeted the affluent American market, emphasising its high standards of service and the fact that it included within its territory much of Britain's finest heritage, history and landscape. The GWR publication, *Historic Sites and Scenes of England*, A. M. Broadley, 1904 (and four subsequent editions to 1934), was an excellent example of this, being written primarily for the American market as a celebration of England and Wales; their history and traditions, GWR style.

The company's own publication: *GWR Ports and Harbours* 1935, offered a summary history of the docks, making particular reference to the historical dimension, and Plymouth's distinguished past, whilst obviously celebrating the achievements of a modern commercial port. The following extract from the GWR history reflects this, the company being most willing and able to promote its own best interest.

Traffic through Millbay reached its peak during the thirties. In April 1931 for example, the *GWR Magazine* included the following item:

The Ocean Liner traffic dealt with at Plymouth during the year 1930 constitutes a record for this port, 789 liners having called, an increase of 46 compared with the previous year. Passengers landed or embarked reached a total of 43,008, an increase of 2404 over 1929. Arrangements have been made for the S S Majestic, 56,621 tons, the largest liner afloat and the S S Olympic, 46,437 tons, to call at Plymouth during the coming season.

May 18th, 1930, also witnessed the first call of the French liner, "Lafayette", the largest diesel driven vessel afloat. The Mayor, Corporation, members of the Plymouth Chamber of Commerce and representatives of the GWR were received on board by Maurice Tillier, Managing Director of Compagnie Generale Transatlantique. Monsieur Tillier proposed the toast to the prosperity of Plymouth as "the gateway of the West and to England". A new cabin class service by the French Line was also introduced between Plymouth and New York.

Referring back to the *GWR Magazine*, and to details for June 1935, there was coverage of another significant event – the world's largest liner calling at Plymouth. The item is included here in full, the Company making the most of such prestigious events:

June 12 was a memorable day in the history of Plymouth, when the world's largest liner entered the Sound. Having achieved a record by passing Bishop Rock, Scilly Isles, 4 days 3 hours 25 minutes after leaving the Ambrose Light-ship, New York, the new giant French Liner 'Normandie' anchored in Plymouth Sound at 10.45 am. The ship, which has the colossal tonnage of 79,000, had on board approximately 1,600 passengers, in addition to her crew of a thousand.

That morning the weather conditions were very exceptional for the time of the year. A strong south-westerly gale was blowing, but by that time the liner had been manoeuvred inside the breakwater the sun was shining brilliantly, and the debarkation of passengers for England was effected under calm conditions.

The Great Western Railway Company's four tenders, "Sir Richard Grenville", "Sir John Hawkins", "Sir Francis Drake" and "Sir Walter Raleigh", steamed alongside. As anticipated, it was found necessary to place small lighters between the tenders, working for'ard, and the liner, as the hull was so curved that the overhanging bow would otherwise have fouled the masts of the tenders.

Captain Rene Pugnet, commander of the "Normandie", received on board his magnificent ship the Mayors of Plymouth, Torquay and Penzance; and a reception was held in one of the spacious saloons of this floating palace, when the Mayor of Plymouth extended to the liner a civic welcome, and congratulated the captain on his wonderful achievement.

On this occasion the majority of the passengers on board were for the Continent, but 358 for this country left the ship at Plymouth. Nearly a thousand bags of Post Office mails were brought ashore by one of the tenders.

Two special boat trains were standing on the Great Western lines adjacent to the dockside in readiness and quickly after the passengers' baggage, which was very considerable, had passed through the hands of the Customs officers and had been stowed in the baggage vans on the trains, and the three hundred passengers who were bound for the Metropolis were seated, the last stage of the race from New York to London was commenced.

The first train was formed exclusively of luxurious saloons thus enabling the American visitors to complete their journey in surroundings comparable with their previous four days afloat. The train, drawn by the engine "Dynevor Castle", accomplished a record run. Docks to Paddington in 3 hours 38 minutes. The passengers, who had the good fortune to travel by this Special were most eulogistic, and many were heard to remark that although they had travelled the world over, they had never experienced such a wonderful journey. They commented particularly on the smooth running.

The second train also provided a brilliant finish to the voyage by occupying four minutes under the four hours on the journey.

It is expected that this leviathan of the ocean

# PLYMOUTH.

Plymouth is the Gateway into England from the Atlantic Ocean. Famous for centuries as the port of departure for maritime adventure into all parts of the world, it is now the most convenient port of arrival for passengers to England and Europe. Its geographical position with its vast and sheltered harbour at the entrance of the English Channel, makes it the natural port for liners from all parts of the world.

Probably the most memorable happening in the history of the Port is its association with the arrival and the defeat of the Spanish Armada, in 1588.

Plymouth's name was also well to the fore during the Civil War, and the success of the Roundheads in the west was principally due to the stubbornness with which the town held out during a series of sieges and blockades by the King's most able generals. When Charles II came to the throne in 1649 he built the Citadel on the eastern end of the Hoe, ostensibly as a defence against foreign invasion, but more probably to overawe the townspeople, in case there was any recurrence of rebellion.

Numerous other events in the history of England are associated with Plymouth, amongst which are the sailing of the "Mayflower" for New England and the voyages of Captain Cook to Australia and New Zealand. The "Mayflower," a little barque of 180 tons —a mere cobble beside the vessels of to-day—sailed from Plymouth in 1620, and when the Pilgrims landed on the barren shores of Massachusetts Bay they named the spot "New Plymouth," in memory of the last port at which they touched the Old World.

At Plymouth the Great Western Railway Company own the principal commercial wet docks. They are situate at Millbay, to the west of the famous Hoe, and between the Hoe and the Government Naval Dockyards at Devonport, which lie farther west again.

Plymouth Sound is one of the most splendid of Britain's natural waterways, and by the construction of the immense breakwater, stretching for a mile across the Sound, which was commenced in 1812, and completed in 1841, at a cost of about £1,500,000, the Harbour of Plymouth was placed among the safest of our ocean ports. In the approaches and entrance to the Great Western Docks, therefore, vessels have the advantage of the conditions of safety provided by the great harbour.

The docks consist of an outer harbour of about 30 acres, entered direct from the Sound without the necessity of any lock gates, and an inner basin of 13 acres. Between the outer harbour and inner basin there is a communication passage 80 feet wide, with a depth of 25 feet. Two pairs of gates are provided in this junction, and these serve not as a lock but, when necessary, to prevent in the inner basin the variations of level of water caused by tides. The outer harbour is naturally subject to the fluctuations in depth of the tides, but Plymouth is fortunate in that these variations are small.

Dealing first with the outer basin, the depth of water available is no less than 28 feet L.W.O.S.T. On the eastern side, and at the seaward end, lies the Millbay Pier. It is here that the ocean passenger and mails traffic is dealt with. The Company's tenders —first-class steamers maintained in the highest state of efficiency and general condition—run between the docks and the great ocean liners anchored in the Sound, and on reaching the Dock are berthed on the north, or dock side, of the pier. Thus the shortest practicable distance between the liner and the shore is utilised, the tender runs straight into a special berth, and the passengers and mails are immediately landed. Mails are dealt with by a modern electric belt conveyor, and the Company have erected an electric travelling crane of 25 cwt. capacity. Adjoining the pier are spacious waiting and refreshment rooms and baggage examination halls, from alongside which the express trains depart. The waiting-room accommodation has just been modernised by the provision of a spacious hall, provided with every up-to-date requirement for ocean travellers. Passengers emerge after the Customs' examination of their luggage to the rail-side and board the train direct. The mails are also quickly loaded up, and at once the journey to London or other parts of the country is commenced in a Great Western train— that is, in perfect comfort with the greatest possible speed. The special trains from Plymouth to Paddington have, on numerous occasions, accomplished the journey of 227 miles in less than four hours.

The advantages of Plymouth as a port of call for ocean liners are being increasingly recognised. It is the westernmost of the large ports on the south coast, and this, combined with the Company's excellent train service to and from London and other parts of the country, enables a substantial saving of time to be effected on the total sea and land journey.

The important development of Plymouth as a port of call for ocean liners is the result of the greater steamship lines making it the first port of call on the eastward journey from America.

The first of these were "The French Line" and the Cunard Company, which adopted Plymouth as the first English port on the trip from the States and Canada. The steamers enter Plymouth Sound before proceeding to the French and other English ports. Passengers for England are thereby enabled, in reaching, say, London or other places, to save practically a whole day as compared with the former arrangements. Other great steamship lines whose vessels regularly call at the port with, or to embark, passengers and mails are the Cunard-White Star, United States Lines, North German Lloyd, Holland American, P. and O. Steam Navigation Company, Orient Line, Elder Dempster Lines, Ltd., British India Steamship Company, Royal Nederlands Steamship Co., Royal Mail Lines, Ltd., Ellerman's City Line, Hall Line, Henderson Line, Hamburg-American, Ellerman and Bucknell, Johnston Line, American Merchant Line, Pacific Steam Navigation Co., Blue Star Line, Bibby Line, Jamaica Direct Fruit Line, Hamburg South American Line, and the New Zealand Shipping Co.

Plymouth was chosen as the arrival port for the "Normandie," which arrived there on her maiden trip on 12th June, 1935, after crossing from New York in record time, and the "Queen Mary" has also made several calls at the port.

North of the Millbay Pier, and on the eastern side of the Outer Dock, there is a very fine floating pontoon, which is available as an extra landing place for passengers and mails. From here also the Company's steamers run passenger trips in the summer season to the many points of beauty and historic interest for which Plymouth is such a convenient centre.

On the same side also is Trinity Pier, a jetty of solid construction, equipped with transit sheds. At this pier is handled the extensive traffic with the Continental ports in fruit and general goods. For instance, a very large proportion of the country's importation of strawberries from France passes through Plymouth. Other quay berths are available on the remainder of the east side for loading and discharging small vessels.

On the opposite side of the Outer Dock is the west wharf, 750 feet in length, providing deep-water berths for the largest cargo steamers, and equipped with first-class hydraulic cranes and commodious transit sheds. Here many of the valuable cargoes of grain brought to England from South America, Canada, etc., are discharged, as well as a considerable part of the fruit traffic.

The Inner Dock is practically a rectangle, being 1,200 feet long (east to west) by 500 feet in width. The depth of water generally is from 17 feet on ordinary neap tides to 22 feet on ordinary spring tides. These depths have, however, been increased at certain points by dredging, and there is now 24½ feet in the deep-water berth at H.W.O.S.T. and 21 feet at H.W.O.N.T. The quays are equipped with hydraulic, electric, and steam cranes, railway lines, and goods sheds, and all varieties of cargoes can be handled. There is a 25-ton hydraulic crane on the south side available for heavy lifts.

A Commercial Graving Dock, owned by the Company, is entered from the inner dock. The entrance is 80 feet wide, the length of the Graving Dock is 454 feet, and the depth over the blocks is greater than that obtaining in the inner wet dock, as previously shown. Owners of vessels using the dry dock have the opportunity of arranging with whatever firms they please to carry out repairs.

Plymouth Docks form a most favourable shipping point for general imports to and exports from the south-western district of England. The docks are conveniently situated in the closest proximity to the central business district of the town.

The number of calls made at Plymouth by Ocean Liners and the large numbers of passengers and mails passing through the port indicate clearly that the advantages of Plymouth as a port of call for Ocean Liners to and from all parts of the world are being increasingly recognised. To deal satisfactorily with the liner traffic, the Company have provided two new tenders, the "Sir John Hawkins" and "Sir Richard Grenville," which, together with the "Sir Francis Drake" and "Sir Walter Raleigh," make a total of four tenders at Plymouth. These tenders are constructed and fitted throughout on the most modern lines, giving ample deck accommodation for passengers' baggage, mails, and motor cars, and spacious and luxurious saloons are provided for the passengers. Mails are landed expeditiously from the tenders by means of a conveyor belt appliance.

An 'up' *Ocean Liner* service leaving Plymouth behind 'Manor' No. 7814, *Fringford Manor* piloting 'Castle' No. 4077 *Chepstow Castle* on 5 July 1955. North Road's flat-topped East Box together with remnants of the old station, to the left, on the 'down' side, can be seen here.

*R. C. Riley*

An 'up' *Ocean Liner* service to Paddington at Aller Junction, Newton Abbot on 18 July 1958, complete with Ocean Liner saloons, for a French Line Special. 'Manor' No. 7820 *Dinmore Manor* and 'Castle' No. 5075 *Wellington* run into Newton Abbot, where the pilot will be removed.

*R. C. Riley*

will pay a visit to Plymouth every two or three weeks henceforth, and when the weather is favourable the tenders will probably work alongside the liner in Cawsand Bay, to the mutual advantage of passengers proceeding to London and Paris.

In addition to the "Normandie", two other large liners arrived at Plymouth from New York early the same morning, viz., the flagship of the Holland America Line, S.S. "Statendam", and the United States Lines' S.S. "Washington", also the City Line S.S. "City of Baroda" from India. Over 600 passengers and 2,500 bags of mail were landed from these three ships, and four Great Western Railway special trains were run from the docks to Paddington.

The remarkable influx of overseas visitors necessitated exceptional catering arrangements, and eight kitchen and restaurant cars which had been provisioned the previous night were included in the boat trains to meet the requirements of the passengers en route.

The advantages of Plymouth as a port of call for ocean liners are being increasingly recognised. It is the westernmost of the large ports on the south coast, and this fact, combined with the Great Western Company's excellent train service to and from Paddington, as exemplified above, enables a substantial saving of time to be effected on the total sea and land journey.

Britain's answer to the "Normandie" was, of course, the legendary Cunard Liner "Queen Mary". Prior to the outbreak of war, this great ship visited Plymouth on many occasions, calling off-shore, no less than nine times in 1938, for example. The first of its visits was that of 15 March 1937. Arriving in brilliant sunshine at 11.05 am the "Queen Mary" was met by the four tenders, Captain Peel received the Lord Mayor of Plymouth on board and 351 passengers were landed. Two Ocean Liner express services awaited them at the docks for Paddington. The first, of 326 tons, and headed by 4-6-0 No. 5016, "Montgomery Castle", left at 2.07 pm with an overall journey time of 3 hours 51 minutes. No 5011, "Tintagel Castle", took the second train of 412 tons in 4 hours 5 minutes.

Accommodation at Millbay was modernised and extended in 1936, part of the larger programme for the West Country, set out in 1935, and a further reflection of prosperity and progress. Refurbishment offered accommodation for 400 people; the waiting area comprising a buffet, ticket offices, postal, cable and luggage handling facilities and currency exchange counters. Decorative details were intended to express harmony, style and modern comforts, as described by the GWR Magazine:

The room is decorated in cream and green, the walls being of cream tiles. The furniture is of light oak with green leather upholstery, while the floor is covered with a green and grey check linoleum in tone with the general colour scheme.

Seating accommodation was provided for 170, the building being air-conditioned.

An earlier proof of the prestige and status given to the ocean liner traffic came with the specially-built super saloons of 1931. Pullman services had been introduced between Paddington and Torbay – 'The Torquay Pullman' ran for two seasons, from 8 July 1929 to 22 September 1930 – and they were also introduced on the Ocean Liner services for a short time in 1929, but the super saloons made the greatest impact. Named after members of the Royal Family, the saloons were resonant of hierarchy, luxury and prestige. This much was celebrated by the GWR Magazine in 1935:

These saloons provide the acme of luxury travelling for railway passengers and are worthy of their names. The interior decorations are beautifully carried out, the saloons and coupe compartments being panelled in highly polished natural light, French walnut veneer, with dark figured burr walnut pilasters on panels between the windows. Above window level is a French walnut coving, running into a panelled flat stippled vellum ceiling, and all the interior doors have a border of French Walnut, with panels of burr walnut. In the ceiling are concealed electric lights covered with satin faced glass panels in bronze frames, which are finished flush with the ceiling, and additional lights are affixed to each end panel of the saloons. The chairs are of the winged type and are upholstered in brown patterned moquettes, with cushions, while heavy pile carpets cover the floor.

Eight such ambassadors of GWR enterprise were provided for ocean liner service, "King George", and "Queen Mary" being the first two to be completed.

The post-war years saw the steady decline of ocean liner traffic, mirrored in the reduction of the tenders – from four which met the "Queen Mary" in 1937, to two, by the end of 1953. "Sir Walter Raleigh" was withdrawn early in 1947; "Sir Francis Drake", in 1953. "Sir John Hawkins", built for the GWR service in 1929, was withdrawn in January 1962; "Sir Richard Grenville", the last of the tenders, entering service in 1931 was, likewise, withdrawn in October 1963. Southampton had ultimately triumphed over Plymouth; the former's deep-water facilities proving a more attractive prospect than the tendering arrangements at Plymouth. Thus ended the long-standing rivalry between the two ports dating back through the previous mid-century, and, with it, a fascinating, stylish and colourful era in Plymouth's ever-eventful history.

Charting the post-war decline, Grahame Farr in his excellent work *West Country Passenger Steamers,* included the following:

In 1957 there were only 154 liner calls and the number still fell each year. The last straw came at the end of 1961 when the "Liberte" called for the last time. The French Line had a long-standing connection with Plymouth, dating from 1875, and towards the end their ships accounted for 72 per cent of all liner calls. . .

A relief 'down' *Torbay Express* passes Burlescombe in East Devon headed by 'King' No. 6015 *King Richard III* on 15 September 1946. Doubtless there were many aboard this train anxious for their long deferred and much missed Evon holiday by the sea. *Pursey Short*

A new era: austerity England on holiday! Dawlish welcomes post-war visitors as the GWR works out its last years. This fascinating photograph of 6 September 1945 sees 'Castle' No. 5028, *Llantillio Castle*, passing the resort on a 'down' express. Bathers are back in possession of the beach but the wartime defences are still in place. *Pursey Short*

## Chapter Five
# Post-War Picture

The immediate post-war world of Austerity meant that there would be no swift return to pre-war standards and service; no further consideration of ideas, as in 1938, – some said a bluff – to electrify the system west of Taunton; no prestigious innovations.

In an article for the *News of the World,* in May 1947, and reprinted in the *GWR Magazine,* Sir James Milne, General Manager, set out the problems for the Company in providing sufficient holiday trains. He noted the cut of 25 per cent from pre-war levels of service, but also announced that due to coal shortages the summer timetable for 1947 had to be reduced by 10 per cent on 1946. The General Manager outlined a depressing scenario of long queues to get into stations and queueing again to board the trains, all this with the prospect for many harassed passengers of standing in corridors in grossly overloaded conditions for long, tiring journeys. Poor timekeeping with the inevitable speed restrictions "made necessary by the lack of new rails and sleepers, and by the priority to be given to the movement of coal traffic," brought additional, unfortunate trials.

Earlier, on 15 March, 1947, the Great Western took the drastic step of temporarily withdrawing the Cornish Riviera Express. This was but one of many services, albeit, the most prestigious, to be affected by the coal crisis; the saving of the vital coal supplies over the Easter period being the explanation for this. It was restored on 16 June.

Nationalisation in 1948 brought little outward change. With seemingly minimum disruption, one set of managers was exchanged for another; one owner for another. The same staff, stock and infrastructure prevailed. In terms of the holiday trade, its essential character, conduct and code was largely retained, except that the late forties and fifties saw ever increasing numbers of people taking the opportunity for holidays. Both in terms of railway operations and the nature of tourism itself, the early sixties reflected a much greater sense of a watershed, i.e. the Beeching Plan, the motor car and the conspicuous rise of the foreign holiday. Things did not happen overnight, but there was radical change by the late sixties.

Holiday traffic to the West Country peaked in the mid to late fifties. The phenomenal scale of services to Torbay has been referred to earlier and probably best represents the popularity of the region at that time. It was also significant that the final stages of the former GWR plan for Paignton/Goodrington were implemented as late as 1957. By that time the road bridge to replace the Tanner's Road level crossing was in place, likewise extra carriage sidings, a turntable and an extended modern station at Goodrington. This was very much the swan-song.

Steam working was dramatically reduced by late 1962 and eliminated during 1964. Diesel power made its effective debut on 22 April, 1958 when the North British Warship Class diesel hydraulic, D600, 'Active' worked the 4.50 a.m. Plymouth-Penzance, returning with the 'up' Cornish Riviera Express as far as Plymouth. Thereafter, it worked the down CRE to Penzance, returning again to Plymouth that night on the up

'Postal'. This locomotive first visited Plymouth on 19 March. Newton Abbot relinquished its steam allocation in January 1963; Exeter followed later that year, in October. Laira lost its last steam locomotives in the Spring of 1964 and Taunton, likewise, during the early Autumn.

By this time, of course, branch line closures were also much apparent. Leaving aside the early closure of the Yealmpton branch in July 1930, and its wartime reopening, 3 November 1941 – 7 October 1947, the first post-war casualty was the Princetown Branch, on 5 March 1956. Two years later the Teign Valley and Dart Valley lines carried their last passengers, or so it seemed in the latter's case. The Teign Valley route between Exeter and Heathfield closed on 9 June 1958; the Totnes-Buckfastleigh line on 1 November that year. Four months later passenger traffic to Moretonhampstead succumbed, closure being on 2 March 1959. The Tavistock and Launceston branch, the last offering branch line access to Dartmoor, ceased on 31 December 1962. By early summer, 1963, the Brixham branch was no-more. Closure here came on 13 May to be followed by the Kingsbridge branch into the South Hams, where services ceased on 16 September 1963.

Closures continued in the autumn of 1963 when the focus turned to East Devon. The beautiful Exe Valley line from Stoke Cannon, northward through Tiverton to Dulverton on the Taunton-Barnstaple branch, closed on 7 October 1963. Tiverton's original rail link from Tiverton Junction on the Taunton-Exeter main line closed one year later, on 5 October 1964. Further eastward, the once important and lengthy branches from Taunton to Barnstaple, and to Minehead closed on 3 October 1966 and 4 January 1971, respectively. On the south coast, the Paignton-Kingswear line was officially closed on 28 October 1972 and handed over to the Dart Valley Railway Company, its new owner. This company had earlier reopened the Dart Valley line in April 1969.

The main line had also experienced considerable change over this period. All intermediate stations between Plymouth and Totnes, with the exception of Brent, closed on 2 March 1959; Brent followed on 5 October 1964. The latter was a significant date for Devon and West Somerset generally, as it also marked the end for intermediate stations between Taunton and Exeter, with the exception of Tiverton Junction.

This litany of gathering decline was in stark contrast with the pattern of progress and investment thirty years earlier. Leaving aside the war years, these three decades represented the high-water mark, the apotheosis of railways and the holiday trade, not only in the West of England, but to all parts of Britain. Preservation, in the form of the two lines to the sea – the West Somerset Railway, to Minehead, and the Torbay Steam Railway, working the Kingswear branch from Paignton, offers atmosphere and memories. So, too, does the Dart Valley line, but the great days have gone.

Looking at the Great Western's record and its legacy in both its railway and related maritime interests, it is clear that in comparative terms the thirties, fifties and sixties were very different decades. Whilst the thirties were definitive of investment and progress, a period of

Princetown: No. 4410 waits to leave for Yelverton in May 1955.                    *P. Q. Treloar*

The terminus at Moretonhampstead seen here in 1958, the year before its closure to passengers. 2-6-2T 5100 Class No. 5168 waits with a return service to Newton Abbot; the South Devon Railway overall roof remained a feature at the station until the end. Together with all the obvious attractions of the eastern aspect of the Moor, Moretonhampstead also boasted the GWR Manor House Hotel, with its golf course and private trout stream.                    *P. Q. Treloar*

substantial growth, confidence and purpose for tourist traffic, the sixties were, indeed, terminal times. Much of the former Great Western empire diminished rapidly during this latter period, whereas, superficially, the fifties appeared secure giving little serious indication of what was so soon to follow. For this reason the 1950s are frequently regarded as some sort of golden age, preserving the best of pre-war achievement in the context of the post-war world. In retrospect, and shorn of the immediate post-war austerity, the fifties were something of a delightful semblance, having the structure and image of prosperity and continuity without the real means and substance to sustain it.

By way of illustration, here we could point to the fact that significant investment was put into ocean terminal accommodation as late as 1952; likewise, the example given earlier, of the money and time directed to the provision of a turntable and extra sidings at Goodrington in connection with the tourist trade, implemented as late as 1957. They were both anachronisms; the vital energy and the circumstances that had driven and sustained the GWR had, like the company itself, passed into history.

Harold Macmillan's famous speech, early in 1960, on "The Winds of Change" applied to more, much more, than its specific, intended reference: the grand question of Britain and its revised world role. On a less exalted level, "the winds of change" were blowing through the railway network.

An extract from the *Railway Magazine* for April 1957, the final reference here, focused directly upon melancholy circumstances, marking the crisis of confidence for the railways generally.

The doubts about the efficiency of the railways appear to have been strengthened by events since the rationing of fuel oils came into force. Although there has been an increase in both passenger and freight traffic, it has been suggested that the railways were not fully prepared to meet the emergency. Many of these criticisms may have been ill-founded, but there have been complaints of over-long transits in freight, and of unpunctual passenger services. Moreover, many people who have been obliged during recent weeks to consign goods or to travel by rail have not found the services sufficiently attractive to make them wish to continue after supplies of oil became more plentiful. Vigorous efforts are being made to improve services, but it must be clear that every possible opportunity must be taken to restore confidence in the railways, and to overcome this reluctance to make full use of them.

For better or worse, this was the reality of the late fifties; the consequences are all too apparent today.

Brent, junction for Kingsbridge and the magnificent South Hams district, as 'Hall' No. 4927 *Farnborough Hall* heads the 7.55 a.m. Penzance-Swansea on 15 July 1958.

*R. C. Riley*

Exeter St. Davids in the early autumn of 1959, a time of transition. 4575 Class 2-6-2T No. 5524 waits at platform 1 with a Kingswear stopping service, held whilst the late running *Cornish Riviera Express* (down) passes on the through road. The express is headed by 'Modified Hall', No. 6995 *Benthall Hall*, of Taunton shed, hauling a failed North British diesel hydraulic 'Warship' Class D601 *Ark Royal*. Steam coming to the rescue of the new diesels was a familiar occurrence in the late fifties and early sixties. 26 September 1959.

*P. Q. Treloar*

West Exe Halt, a southern suburb of Tiverton, saw a good crowd on Bank Holiday Monday, 5 August, 1963. Not all the passengers seem to trust to the seasonal weather, but it is a fascinating, almost final image of holiday traffic from this Halt, and, indeed, the entire line, as it closed on 7 October that year. West Exe was opened on 19 March, 1928. *P. Gray*

Buckfastleigh, very different in 1958 from what it is now as home to steam on the Dart Valley line. In this view, from 11 October 1958, 1400 Class 0-4-2T No. 1427 leaves with the 11.15 a.m. service from Ashburton to Totnes. A camping coach can be seen in the station yard. Note also the pagoda-style shelter immediately behind the locomotive. Within a month of this photograph being taken, the line was closed to passengers; it reopened as a privately preserved branch in April 1969. *P. Gray*

The returning Sunday School day excursion to Teignmouth ready to leave on its final stage home to Buckfastleigh, on 29 June 1960. 4500 Class 2-6-2T Nos. 4555 and 4561, both now preserved, and working in the West Country, are seen here at the 'down' platform at Totnes from where the train has reversed and will cross the main line to gain access to the branch, east of the station, on the 'up' side.

*P. Gray*

Great Western revisited. 2-6-2T No 4555, now sporting a copper-capped chimney, arrives at Churston en-route to Kingswear, 22 April 1993. No longer the junction for Brixham, Churston retains a good deal of its former character, albeit with certain concessions to our modern world.

*Author*